POEMS OF AMBROSE BIERCE

POEMS OF AMBROSE
BIERCE

EDITED AND INTRODUCED BY M. E. GRENANDER

UNIVERSITY OF NEBRASKA PRESS: LINCOLN AND LONDON

A truncated version of the editor's
introduction
is forthcoming in the *Garland
Encyclopedia of
American Nineteenth-Century Poetry.*

© 1995 by the
University of Nebraska Press.
All rights reserved.
Manufactured in the United
States of America.
The paper in this book meets
the minimum require-
ments of American National
Standard for In-
formation Sciences – Perma-
nence of Paper
for Printed Library Materials,
ANSI Z39.48-1984.
Library of Congress Catalog-
ing in Publication Data
Bierce, Ambrose, 1842–1914?
[Poems]
Poems of Ambrose Bierce / ed-
ited and intro-
duced by M. E. Grenander.
p.   cm.
Includes bibliographical ref-
erences (p.) and
index. ISBN 0-8032-1246-1
I. Grenander, M. E.
(Mary Elizabeth), 1918– .
II. Title. PS1097.A6
1995   811'.4–dc20 94-13761
CIP

Contents

Introduction

Ambrose Bierce has always hovered on the margins of America's literary canon. And even there, his place has been secured by his short stories and the epigrammatic definitions in his *Devil's Dictionary*. Most readers will be startled to learn that he wrote any poetry at all. Hence I was not only gratified but also mildly surprised at being invited to contribute an essay on Bierce to the *Garland Encyclopedia of American Nineteenth-Century Poetry*, a commentary on the Library of America's anthology, for Bierce's inclusion in these volumes meant that his verses were at last entering the mainstream of American literature. This introduction is an expansion of the essay I wrote for the *Garland Encyclopedia*, and the poems that follow it greatly outnumber the selections in the Library of America anthology. For Bierce, despite his own disclaimers, *was* a poet, one who occupies a unique niche in nineteenth-century American verse. According to the sole modern commentator on his work in this area of literature, Donald Sidney-Fryer, Bierce as poet has "remained almost unknown," although he "clearly merits the attention of the discriminating lover and student of poetry" (11).

Born June 24, 1842, on a farm in Meigs County, Ohio, Bierce in 1846 moved with his family to northern Indiana, where, except for a brief sojourn in 1859 as a student at the Kentucky Military Institute, he grew up and attended high school. During these years the United States was being torn apart by what remains its darkest tragedy, the legal bondage in the South of men, women, and children of color. An idealistic youth, Bierce worked for an antislavery newspaper in the Hoosier state, and in 1861, when the national tensions exploded in the Civil War, the teenager enlisted as a private in the Ninth Indiana Infantry Regiment. As he advanced in rank, he asked for assignment as a field officer in charge of black troops, although he later canceled the request and instead became a topographical engineer acting as a staff officer. He greatly admired the bravery and prowess of black soldiers in action when he observed them at the Battle of Nashville on December 15–16, 1864.

He was an exemplary soldier during his four years' military service for the Union, participating in some of the most famous battles in the Western theater of operations, and he was discharged a first lieutenant in 1865. After a stint in Alabama as a U.S. Treasury aide, he joined his Civil War commanding officer, Gen. William B. Hazen, on a military expedition through Indian country from Omaha to San Francisco. There, in 1867, failing to get the captaincy he had been promised (although he was later breveted to the rank of major), he resigned from Hazen's team and began training himself as a writer. His poems and prose appeared in various publications, including Bret Harte's *Overland Monthly.* His courtship of a beautiful California heiress, Mary Ellen ("Mollie") Day, is reflected in the uncollected poems "To Thee, My Darling," with its charming pun on Mollie's last name, and "Serenade," with "Rosalie" perhaps being the first. Ambrose and Mollie were married on December 25, 1871, and in the spring of 1872, they left San Francisco for London.

Bierce spent three congenial years in England, and he remained an Anglophile all his life. Unlike Mark Twain, he moved in journalistic rather than literary circles there. Nevertheless, his first three books were published in London: in 1873, *The Fiend's Delight* and *Nuggets and Dust* and in 1874, *Cobwebs from an Empty Skull*. His two sons, Day and Leigh, were born in England. But Bierce's wife was not as happy there as her husband. In April 1875, pregnant with their third child, Mollie returned to San Francisco with their young sons; Bierce joined them in October in time for the birth of a daughter, Helen.

Bierce resumed his journalistic career on the West Coast, interrupted only by his backbreaking (and heartbreaking) participation in a Black Hills mining venture. He took a giant leap into prominence when William Randolph Hearst hired him in 1887 to write for the *San Francisco Examiner*. Hearst paid Bierce well and gave him carte blanche on his contributions, and almost all of his most famous work appeared initially in the *Examiner*.

The years from 1887 to 1899 were the most significant in Bierce's life. His marriage turned to ashes when, in 1888, he discovered that Mollie had been the recipient of some ardent letters from a distinguished Danish admirer. Although there was no serious impropriety on her part, she had been the not unwilling recipient of these indiscreet missives. Bierce's reaction was to leave her, never to return. Both he and Mollie, with admirable dignity and reserve, refrained from any public comment on the breakup of their marriage. Hence one of his poems, "Oneiromancy," is of particular biographical interest, since it may have been a veiled expression of the intense grief he felt over what he perceived as his betrayal by the woman he loved. Poetry may have offered Bierce an outlet for feelings that he could express in no other way.

In any event, his anguish over the separation from his wife and the death of his oldest son in a gun duel over a young woman was transmuted into the writing of some of Bierce's greatest stories, collected in 1892 and 1893, under the titles *In the Midst of Life (Tales of Soldiers and Civilians)* and *Can Such Things Be?* Moreover, he composed numerous satirical verses against California rogues and fools, which were assembled in *Black Beetles in Amber* (1892). From 1895 to 1898 his articles scoring America's enthusiasm for the Spanish-American War appeared in the *San Francisco Examiner* despite Hearst's militant jingoism. One of Bierce's great journalistic coups on behalf of Hearst also occurred during this period, when he was sent to Washington, D.C., in 1896 on a temporary assignment to spearhead the *Examiner's* attack against Congressional passage of Collis Huntington's railroad funding bill. Successful in this effort, Bierce left California permanently for the East in 1899, settling in Washington, where he lived for the rest of his life. In 1903 he published a second book of poems, *Shapes of Clay,* and in 1906 *The Cynic's Word Book,* as *The Devil's Dictionary* was initially titled.

During most of his years in Washington, Bierce continued to write for Hearst's newspapers and for his *Cosmopolitan* magazine. In 1909 he resigned and began to prepare his twelve-volume *Collected Works* (cw), the source of poems and essays included in this anthology. It was completed in 1912; the next year Bierce wound up his affairs and, in October, left Washington on the first stages of a trip that he planned would take him through Mexico to South America. After revisiting the battlefields of his Civil War days, he crossed the Texas border from El Paso to Juarez, where he was given credentials to join the army of Pancho Villa as an observer.

Villa, who was leading a populist rebellion in Mexico against the reactionary government of Gen. Victoriano Huerta, had occupied Chihuahua on December 8. Bierce's last letter, written from Chihuahua on December 26, 1913, states that he intended to join the Villista forces in Ojinaga the next day. On January 11, 1914, there was a fierce battle in Ojinaga during which, scholars believe, on the basis of circumstantial evidence, Bierce was killed and his corpse destroyed in a mass cremation to prevent the spread of typhus.

Bierce's poetry constituted only a fraction of his total output. He did not consider himself a poet, regarding the true poet as the "king of men," whose output was the "highest, ripest, richest fruit" of all human endeavors (*CW* 10:249–50). Creation of poetry was its own reward, as he noted in "To a Dejected Poet," for the "sacred ministry of song" was "rapture." Bierce's disarmingly modest little verse, "Humility," indicates the place he assigned himself. It is noteworthy, however, that he turned to poetry in one of the last things he wrote, the uncollected "My Day of Life," composed in September, 1910, during a vacation trip he made back to California from his new home in the East.

Bierce's theory of poetry was a complex one, presented in part in several essays in volume 10 of his *Collected Works:* "The Matter of Manner" (57–64); "Edwin Markham's Poems" (137–48); "Who Are Great?" (249–55); "Poetry and Verse" (256–73); and "Thought and Feeling" (274–77). These essays and others are included here under the heading "About Poetry." This section concludes with extracts from some of Bierce's letters about Ezra Pound that give us a charming glimpse of the aging Bierce: toward the end of his life, still doing what he could to encourage a young poet he considered promising (as indeed he had done throughout his career).

Although poetry was "too multiform and many-sided" to define dogmatically, Bierce wrote (*cw* 10:260), it could be recognized by the discerning reader. It was a complex amalgam of emotion, imagination, and thought. When a poet has a profound thought, he must "express it so as to produce an emotion in an emotional mind," as Coleridge does in "Kubla Khan," which addresses "not the intellect, but the heart" (10:274, 277). "It is the philosopher's trade to make us think, the poet's to make us feel. If he is so fortunate as to have his thought, well and good; he can make us feel, with it as well as without—and without it as well as with" (10:274). To achieve the poetic effect on the reader, the poet, in his turn, must have imagination, the "supreme and almost sufficient literary endowment," the divine gift that makes life "picturesque, enchanting, astonishing, terrible" (10:239, 245). In the poem it takes the form of imagery, which is "not only the life and soul of poetry; it is the poetry" (10:196).

Nevertheless, although poetry and thought are not essentially connected and demand separate consideration, great poetry commonly has both (*cw* 10:275–76). "No elevated composition has the right to be called great if the message that it delivers is neither true nor just. All poets, even the little ones, are feelers, for poetry is emotional; but all the great poets are thinkers as well" (10:141–42). Two of Bierce's very short poems are extraordinary exemplars of profound philosophical concepts powerfully compressed into witty short poems: "A Lacking Factor" and "Two Types." In "A Lacking Factor," he deals with a knotty question in applied ethics that moralists have wrestled with for centuries. By what criteria does one judge the validity of a proposed course of action?

One solution, which philosophers call consequentialism, is to evaluate a decision in terms of its effects when it is carried out. The fatal and obvious flaw of consequentialism, however, is that no one can foretell the future, a problem Bierce returned to again and again in fables, epigrams, and stories, notably in "The Coup de Grâce." "Two Types" is another tightly condensed poetic version of a vexing psychological puzzle that philosophers have examined at length: the nature of courage, which is treated exhaustively by Aristotle in Book III of the *Nichomachaean Ethics*. As Thomas Szasz, the psychiatric scholar and the only successful modern imitator of Bierce, put it in *The Second Sin* (39), "Courage is the willingness to play even when you know the odds are against you." In the three poems "Right," "Infralapsarian," and "Inauspiciously," Bierce deals with what is probably the most fundamental issue in the history of human thought: determinism. It should be recognized here that Bierce grappled with the problem of philosophical necessity—in my view successfully—even though the verses in which he expressed his conclusions are light-hearted ones.

In Bierce's poetic theory, thought, emotion, and imagination have in their turn an intricate relation to the diction through which they are made manifest. Diction is to poetry, Bierce wrote, "what color is to painting. The thought is the outline drawing, which, if it be great, no dauber who stops short of actually painting it out can make wholly mean, but to which the true artist with his pigments can add a higher glory and a new significance" (*cw* 10:258). With the proviso that the noble, poetic idea cannot be reduced to the prosaic by "crude or ludicrous verbiage" any more than fine words masking pauper thought can elevate base or vulgar sentiment (10:258–59), Bierce turns his attention to the "delicate and difficult art" of managing words. Since the best poetry, like the best prose, is "severely simple in diction" (10:260), no one "who knows how to write prose can hold in light esteem an art so nearly allied to his own as that of poetic expression" (10:258). Sidney-Fryer (26) has pointed out that Bierce, in his own poetry, "has a good ear for colloquial speech" and "a good eye for the unexpected and homely detail," anticipating the ironic, colloquial temper of modern poets. Although "a master of the grand manner, . . . in most of his poems he simply uses his own conversational style."

One aspect of diction is verse. But here again the relationship, for Bierce, is not a simple one. The vast majority of readers, he held, regard verse and poetry as strictly synonymous. It is the verse that pleases them; even if it should contain poetry, "they like it none the better for that" (*cw* 10:263). However, the metrical form in which poetry is most accessible is not essential to it. Hence, though all poetry is good, not all verse is good (10:260). "Some of the finest poetry extant . . . is neither metric nor rhythmic" (10:256). Bierce would have been in complete agreement with Norman Maclean's repeated claim that his classic novella, *A River Runs Through It* (1976), was his "poem" to his family.

Still, meter and rhyme, in addition to being easier to understand than poetry, have a basic appeal of their own (*cw* 10:201–2), inducing a sensuous pleasure in readers. Sounds in harmony with the physical organism that perceives them have a natural charm, and meter appeals to the sense of time. Consequently "the old lady who found so much Christian comfort in pronouncing the word 'Mesopotamia' was nobody's fool; the word consists of two pure dactyls." Exemplifying "the satisfaction the ordinary mind takes in mere metre" are "the senseless refrains of popular songs" and

Shakespeare's nonsense verses, which sing themselves, full of "the very spirit of poetry" (10:263–64, 275).

Versification is thus an intricate art embracing "a multitude of dainty wisdoms" (*cw* 10:258). Bierce singled out blank verse as "the most difficult of all metrical forms," Milton being the only poet who has ever mastered it in English. What Shakespeare wrote, Bierce said, was not blank verse but "dramatic blank, a very different thing" (10:141, 209). And iambic pentameter couplets were particularly suited to satire, as demonstrated by Dryden, Pope, and Bierce himself.

Finally, the age in which poets live has practical consequences for their art. Bierce was very much a man of his time in being concerned about the impact of science on contemporary culture, sapping as it did the substructure not only of religion but of art. "I do not regret the substitution of knowledge for conjecture," he wrote, "and doubt for faith; I only say that it has its disadvantages, and among them we reckon the decay of poesy. . . . The world's greatest poets have lived in rude ages, when their races were not long emerged from the night of barbarism" (*cw* 10:270–71). He voiced the same idea in the uncollected poems "Science" and "How Blind Is He" and in the lovely concluding stanza of "Geotheos." He also has fun with it in "Tempora Mutantur."

Science, however, has revealed Nature's secrets "with regard to poetry's materials—the visible and audible without us, and the emotional within—. . . and found them uninteresting to the last degree," narrowing the unknown "to such mean dimensions that imagination has lost her free, exultant stride, and moves with mincing step and hesitating heart" (*cw* 10:269). Nevertheless, poets cannot ignore their intellectual environment. "As a poetical mental attitude, that of doubt is meaner than that of faith, that of speculation less commanding than that of emotion; yet the poet of to-day must assume them" (10:272). Joaquin Miller, being "a rude individual intelligence," would have been in full sympathy with the barbarism of the ancients, but he was an isolated voice in an age of polish.

Tennyson, on the other hand, "the man of culture," full of the disposition of his less than vital time, loyally accepted its hard conditions, touching "with a valid hand the harp which the other beats in vain" (*cw* 10:271–72).

> As inspiration grows weak and acceptance disobedient, form of delivery becomes of great moment; in so far as it can, the munificence of manner must mitigate the poverty of matter; so it occurs that the poets of later life excel their predecessors in the delicate and difficult arts and artifices of versification as much as they fall below them in imagination and power. (*cw* 10:272–73)

These views sound astonishingly modern when read in the light of recent observations by a distinguished contemporary poet, Joseph Brodsky. Dismissing free verse as a "low-calorie diet," Brodsky indicated that "only content can be innovative and . . . formal innovation can occur only within the limits of form. Rejection of form is a rejection of innovation." He then added: "Form is appealing not because of its inherited nobility but because it is a sign of restraint and a sign of strength" (221–22).

A knowledge of Bierce's theory of poetry contributes greatly to an understanding of his own writing in this form. If he was not by his own standards a great poet, he was nevertheless a good one. He was as versatile in the kinds of poetry he wrote as in the rest of his work, his subjects ranging from the cosmic to the particular and local. Representative of the former are "The Passing Show" and "A Vision of Doom," as well as the extraordinary little tercet, "Creation," which Sidney-Fryer (20) regards as Bierce's finest poem, characterizing it as a "masterpiece of boldness and compression."

Metrically, "The Passing Show" and "A Vision of Doom" are different, yet the four-line iambic pentameter stanzas of the first (rhyming *aaba*) and the blank verse of the second are both appropriate to serious verse. What the poet sees is chilling in its bleak despair. It would be a gross oversimplification to characterize these poems as dystopias, for they portray not merely the devolution of a degenerating society, but that of a dying universe. Today, enlightened by the second law of thermodynamics, we can see that Bierce is grappling with the concept of entropy, or, according to one dictionary definition, "the degradation of the matter and energy in the universe to an ultimate state of inert uniformity." But not only is he dealing with this sophisticated scientific formulation in both poems; he is also presenting an equally abstruse philosophical concept: metaphysical idealism. In other words, the dying universe itself has no ontological being; it is a "phantom world" that exists only as "the shadow of a poet's dream."

Other serious poems by Bierce, not on this cosmic scale, deal with his concern over his country's future. His stance was diametrically opposed to the exuberant optimism of Walt Whitman, but it was no less the expression of a deeply felt patriotism. Bierce's most famous poem in this vein— probably the most famous of all his poems—is "Invocation," composed for and read aloud at a San Francisco Fourth of July celebration in 1888. The California poet George Sterling, who wrote a critical introduction to a sumptuous edition of "Invocation" published in 1928 by the Book Club of

California, characterized it as a "great poem, as noble an in-
vocation as we have heard this side of the Atlantic."

The three poems "Invocation," "Freedom," and "To the
Bartholdi Statue" embody a recurrent theme in Bierce's
thinking: his refusal to worship freedom in the abstract.
When it was held up as an ideal, his response was to ask
whose freedom was being advanced to do what? For him,
liberty was a means, not an end to be pursued for its own
sake. This in turn was but one aspect of his adherence to
what today we call situational ethics. Bierce was no ideo-
logue, holding fast to principles regardless of context. He
maintained, rather, that they should always be considered in
the light of circumstances of time and place.

Like "To the Bartholdi Statue," "Invocation" touches on
the threat of anarchism, which with its turn toward violence
at the end of the nineteenth century had drawn the atten-
tion of Henry James and Joseph Conrad as well. "Invoca-
tion" also mentions the Civil War ("The chains we riveted we
broke"), to which Bierce devoted a number of other poems.
These all differ notably from his short stories about the Civil
War. In his fiction, he dealt with the immediacies of its hor-
rors: soldiers (both Federal and Confederate) in the midst of
battle. His poetry, however, reflects the contemplative wis-
dom of an older man looking back on the fiery passages of
his youth; it reflects a serene magnanimity toward a re-
spected fallen foe and even doubts about the wisdom of the
fratricidal conflict.

"The Hesitating Veteran" and "A Year's 'Casualties'" re-
veal Bierce's mature opinion, and, together with "At a 'Na-
tional Encampment,'" refer to the speaker's own old
wounds. "A Year's 'Casualties'" includes an allusion to the
Confederate Gen. Stonewall Jackson's famous dying words

on May 10, 1863, after being wounded by his own men at the Battle of Chancellorsville: "Let us cross over the river and rest under the shade of the trees." Bierce's charity toward the South is presented in both "The Confederate Flags" and "To E. S. Salomon." In the former, he argues for returning the Confederate colors to the troops who had fought under them. And Bierce's address to "General" Salomon (whose title derived from his service in the California National Guard) attacks his protests against decorating the graves of the Confederate dead. Related to his poems on the Civil War are those about the Union's commander in chief and later President: "The Death of Grant" and "Contentment."

Several of Bierce's poems are concise and witty reflections on the international scene, in which the modern reader cannot but be struck by how unerringly he put his finger on the sore spots of the world that are still festering today. "A Voice from Pekin" purports to be a brief monologue by the Manchu dowager empress, Tz'u-hsi, the former concubine who ruled her country from 1862 to 1908. Although she was shrewd and strong-willed, because of the xenophobia she shared with her subjects she was unable to avert her static empire's slide toward helplessness. Grown intolerant of Western influence, China had turned in upon herself and closed her ports to the foreign "barbarians." But the empress, China's last, was no match for the great powers that were determined to pry the valves of this rich oyster apart for the entry of free trade and international relations. From the 1860s on, Western businessmen and evangelical missionaries, following the United States in its "open door" policy, were swarming through China. Benjamin Park Avery, a Californian and, like Bierce, a contributor to the *Overland Monthly,* which he also edited for six months, had been ap-

pointed by President Grant as America's minister plenipo-
tentiary to China in 1874, a post he held with some distinc-
tion until his death in Peking on November 8, 1875. Bierce,
who was living in England at the time, had noted Avery's ap-
pointment with approval.

Bierce's attention had been directed toward France in one
of the oddest passages of his career, recounted by him in the
autobiographical essay "Working for an Empress" (*cw*
1:349–59). In 1874, during his residence in England, he was
recommended by a mutual friend to the widowed Empress
Marie Eugénie, then a wealthy exile living in the London
outpost of Chislehurst, where Napoleon III had died on
January 9, 1873. The ex-Communard Henri Rochefort,
who had published a scurrilous Parisian paper, *La Lanterne*,
that traduced the Second Empire's royal family, was in Eng-
land threatening to bring out his periodical there. To foil
him by copyrighting the title in English, the terrified em-
press hired Bierce to write an expensively produced pub-
lication called *The Lantern*. Bierce was responsible for every
word of the only two issues that appeared, on May 18 and
July 15, 1874. It then ceased publication, after the thwarted
Rochefort left England for Belgium. The verse *"Novum Or-
ganum"* reproduced here appeared in the May 18 issue, al-
though Bierce, who was really a staunch admirer of Eng-
land, subsequently characterized it as "ill-humored."

His poem "France" is a much later expression of his inter-
est in that country and its unstable Third Republic. It can be
dated through internal evidence as having been composed
between 1889 and 1891. "Thy Hugo dead" is Victor Hugo, to
the powers of whose "giant intellect" Bierce alluded in an es-
say ("The Novel," *cw* 10:24); Hugo had died on May 22,
1885. His political advocacy of social justice is known to

many readers through his monumental novel *Les Misérables.*
"[T]hy Boulanger alive" is Georges Ernest Boulanger, a cash-
iered military leader and popular demagogue who had been
elected to the Chamber of Deputies and had lost a duel to
the elderly premier, Charles Floquet. He attempted to
weaken the powers of parliament and strengthen the presi-
dency, an office to which he aspired. However, to the dismay
of his followers he fled to Belgium in March 1889 because he
feared a trial for treason. Hence he would "govern where he
dares not dwell." Since he was regarded as a successor to
Napoleon I and Napoleon III in his efforts to establish him-
self as a powerful dictator, Bierce says he "grabs at the scep-
ter and conceals the chain." He was tried in absentia in
August 1889, for plotting against the republic, and he com-
mitted suicide in Belgium on September 30, 1891.

"A False Prophecy" refers to Dom Pedro II, the states-
manlike sovereign of Brazil for half a century. His 1876 tour
of the United States had included a short stay in San Fran-
cisco, where the staunchly republican Bierce would have no
part of what he regarded as the Bohemian Club's sycophan-
tic adulation of the visiting monarch. But Pedro himself was
a simple man, a wise and enlightened ruler; in manumitting
his country's slaves, he bore comparison with Lincoln in the
United States and the "Czar Liberator," Alexander II, who
had freed Russia's serfs in 1861. Both had been assassinated,
a fate Bierce foretold for Pedro in "A False Prophecy," writ-
ten in 1895 (the year that Bierce appended to the poem
when it was published years later). The Brazilian emperor's
forthright efforts to move his country in the direction of a
secular democracy controlled by civilians aroused the en-
mity of the large landownders, the church, and especially
the army. In 1889 he was the target of a coup led by dis-

affected officers, inaugurating a period of military dictator-
ships for Brazil. Pedro abdicated and, with his family, was
banished to Europe. Consequently when Bierce's poem was
published in *Shapes of Clay* in 1903, the fate it had foretold
for Pedro was a "false prophecy."

In his essay "The Turko-Grecian War" (*CW* 9:287–94),
Bierce's sympathies are clearly with Turkey, whose sultan
from 1876 to 1909 was Abdulhamid II. Bierce's poem "The
Eastern Question," however, is a relatively even-handed
treatment of the conflict. At the Treaty of Berlin ending the
Russo-Turkish War of 1877–78, Thessaly and part of the
Epirus were given to Greece; Crete and Armenia, to Turkey.
In order to hold Armenia within the decrepit Ottoman Em-
pire, the sultan had systematically massacred the Arme-
nians. Fearful of a similar fate, the Christians of Crete re-
volted in 1896–97, declaring war against Turkey and
marching into Thessaly. But their forces were little more
than an undisciplined mob motivated by nationalistic fer-
vor, and they were no match for Abdulhamid's German-
trained troops. In Bierce's words, "They were merely a war-
like people attacking a military people—the worst soldiers
in Europe, without commanders, challenging the best sol-
diers in the world led by two able strategists" (9:290). The
sultan's victory, however, was an empty one. The European
powers, which were all busily engaged in extending their he-
gemony over the Middle East, took Crete away from Turkey
and made it self-governing. In his prose account, Bierce
wrote:

> Indubitably Turkey's doom as a European Power was long
> ago pronounced in the Russian language, but she dies with
> a dignity befitting her glorious history. Foot to foot and

> sword to sword she struggles with the hosts assailing her, now on this side, and now on that. Against attack by her powerful neighbors and insurrection of her heterogeneous provinces, she has manifested a courage, a vitality, a fertility of resource, a continuity and tenacity of purpose which in a Christian nation would command our respect and engage our enthusiasm. (*CW* 9:293)

"The Crime of 1903" refers to the aid given by the United States to Panama, enabling her to secede from Colombia on November 3. Her independence lasted only fifteen days, however. As part of its interventionist policy in Latin America, the United States, in the Panama Canal Treaty of November 18, in effect made Panama its military protectorate, with the unilateral right to intervene there to maintain peace and protect property, to build and operate a canal, and to govern the Canal Zone bisecting Panama. The canal was built in 1914 and celebrated with an international exposition in 1915. The hated Treaty of 1903 remained in place until 1978. In that year, after negotiations that had dragged on since 1964, it was replaced with two new treaties implemented in 1979.

"Saith the Czar" is nominally spoken by Russia's Nicholas II, a first cousin to Great Britain's George V. "After Portsmouth" is an allusion to the Russo-Japanese War of 1904–5. Japan, alarmed at Russia's expansion into Manchuria, had launched a surprise attack against its fleet, which was followed by both naval and military victories for the island empire. President Theodore Roosevelt intervened and mediated the Treaty of Portsmouth, which ended the war, on September 5, 1905, earning the Nobel Peace Prize for his efforts. The signing of the treaty took place at the Portsmouth

Naval Yard in Kittery, Maine, across the Piscataqua River
from Portsmouth, New Hampshire. Russia's minister of fi-
nance, Sergei Witte, acted on behalf of his country. When he
returned home he became Russia's first premier, inaugurat-
ing a constitutional monarchy under Czar Nicholas II. Rus-
sia then entered its period of greatest prosperity. The Social-
ist Revolutionaries, however, continued their terrorist
policies, assassinating thousands of government officials, in-
cluding those at the village level. Nicholas himself was to be
deposed in 1917 (after Bierce's death) and, as the world
knows, was murdered, together with his family, by the Bol-
sheviks in 1918.

Among the shorter serious poems Bierce wrote were a
number of elegiac lyrics, although he took a more playful at-
titude toward this form in the entry under "Elegy" in *The
Devil's Dictionary,* which parodies Thomas Gray's "Elegy
Written in a Country Churchyard." But it was typical of
Bierce to poke fun at practices he himself followed. His ele-
gies, in fact, are among the most charming lyrics he wrote. The
delightful "In Memoriam" will appeal to all ailurophiles. His
impressionistic "A Study in Gray" is a kind of verbal equiva-
lent to Whistler's portrait of his mother. Other poems of his
in this vein are "Another Way" and "Presentiment."

Poetry was an outlet for some of Bierce's deepest and ten-
derest feelings about women. Many years' study of the de-
tails of his life and works has convinced me that the popular
portrait of him as a near-satyr is totally false. To be sure, he
was one of those men (like Benjamin Franklin) who are at-
tracted to women almost without exception, whatever their
age or degree of pulchritude. It was as if he carried in his
heart an ideal of womanhood that was more or less embod-
ied by all women. As they returned his fondness for them,

Bierce had a number of close female friends. In many if not most cases this mutual attraction was carried on largely by correspondence because his chronic asthma forced him to spend much of his life in isolated small mountain villages (like the Auburn of the foothills in his parody of Goldsmith). Some of his sonnets and elegies reveal the closeness of the tie between him and women friends. The poet Ina Coolbrith wrote another friend in 1883 that he had been "kind as a brother" to her, and Lois Rather (16) refers to Bierce's "sweet loyalty and fidelity in his affections for women." He was, however, too fastidious for indiscriminate sex. Basically, I believe, Bierce was a one-woman man, and the woman he loved was the one he married. Nothing so banal as adultery was involved in his breakup with Mollie. But his discovery of the letters she had received (hinted at in "Onei-romancy") revealed that she had not shared his whole-souled devotion. Her death in 1905 was a terrible blow to him, even though they had been separated for many years.

Bierce also wrote moving elegies about his men friends, notably "William F. Smith," "J. F. B.," and "T. A. H." The sonnet "J. F. B." commemorated the death of James F. Bowman, a close friend of his early years. Bowman was a kindly and convivial fellow, editor of *The Californian* and *The Golden Era*, to which Bierce had contributed in 1867 and 1868; his uncollected poems "Basilica" and "A Mystery" both appeared in *The Californian*. Bowman later wrote editorials for the *San Francisco Chronicle*. Something of a philosopher, he was a scholarly skeptic and a student of Anglo-Saxon poetry who hosted Sunday brunches where his guests drank mightily, drew pictures on the tablecloth, and talked endlessly. But he was also a prankster who joined Bierce in playing practical jokes. He founded the Bohemian Club, with Bierce as a charter member and club secretary from 1876 to 1878, when he resigned. Bowman died in 1882.

In quite a different vein is "T. A. H.," Bierce's epitaph on the Englishman Thomas Arundel Harcourt, who wrote accomplished verses and translated Zola. One of the stable of writers maintained by the historian H. H. Bancroft, he had been a co-author with Bierce of a little book called *The Dance of Death,* a best-selling literary hoax purporting to attack the obscene appeal of the waltz. After Harcourt's wife left him for another man, he turned to alcohol. He ended his life by jumping from a window. In the *Examiner* for February 5, 1888 (quoted in Paul Fatout's *Ambrose Bierce: The Devil's Lexicographer,* 143), Bierce wrote of Harcourt that he "went to the everlasting bad through domestic infelicity and foreign brandy, dying in poverty's last ditch upon a golden couch." Bierce had memorialized him in verse in "T. A. H." and a second poem about Harcourt's death, "Reminded."

By far the greatest part of Bierce's output in verse, however, was satire. Here he was going against the grain of the American ethos, as he himself recognized (in his essay "The Passing of Satire," *cw* 10:281–84) and as Charles Dickens had prophesied in *Martin Chuzzlewit* (1843–44). A candid American in Dickens's novel admits that "no satirist could breathe" the air of the United States. "If another Juvenal or Swift could rise up among us to-morrow, he would be hunted down" and subjected to "the foulest and most brutal slander, the most inveterate hatred and intolerant pursuit" (339). Since these words are a pretty accurate forecast of what was to happen in Bierce's case, his beliefs about satire are of particular significance. The theory that it embodied, according to his own accounts, was based on three principles. First, satire should criticize specific individuals, not abstractions. Second, it was a form of punishment, "a terror to all manner of civic and personal unworth" ("The Passing of Satire," *cw* 10:283), a lashing of rascals who, despite Bierce's efforts over a considerable period to reclaim them, "manifested a deplorable, and doubtless congenital, propensity to continuance in sin" (*cw* preface, 5:10). Third, it was the satire itself that would have lasting significance, not its objects. In other words, even if the subjects of satire were obscure, they would achieve a kind of permanence if the verse in which they were pilloried had literary merit. Bierce derived these principles of "applied satire," he said, and its "laws, liberties, and limitations" from "reverent study of the masters" (*cw* preface, 4:10). And, indeed, the influence of Pope and Swift, among others, is easy to track in his satirical verses.

On December 4, 1893, Bierce wrote the Cambridge publishers Stone and Kimball, arguing against their objection to his satire—that it dealt with obscure figures:

It does not appear to be an objection in such works as the "English Bards and Scotch Reviewers," "The Dunciad," and most of the satires which have lived; but of course I am not a Byron nor a Pope. Nevertheless, I cannot see how the quality or interest of a piece is affected by application to a real, though unknown, person instead of presenting it as a general satire, with perhaps a fictitious name. If the verse is good it *makes* the victim known; if not good it is not worth publishing anyhow. (Quoted in Grenander, *Ambrose Bierce*, 61)

Bierce later wrote that he had "done what he could" to dispel the obscurity of the objects of his satire and to award them "such fame as he was able to bestow" (*cw* preface, 5:9).

Bierce characterized himself as a satirist "who does not ac-

cept the remarkable doctrine that while condemning a sin
he should spare the sinner" (*CW* preface, 4:10). In "To a
Censor" he scorns those who attack not specific rascals but
the abstraction Rascality, fearlessly affirming "That wicked-
ness is wrong and sin a vice, / That wrong's not right, nor
foulness ever nice," smiting the offense while sparing the of-
fender. He sounded the same theme in "Substance or
Shadow."

Nevertheless, Bierce himself wrote a few satires on gen-
eral subjects. Among his favorite targets were Christmas (he
was a veritable Scrooge), theosophy, politics (e.g., "The
Statesmen" and "Egotist"), religion ("The New Decalogue,"
"The Binnacle," and "Christian"), dogs (the only animals he
disliked), science, and law. "Judex Jocosus" and "An Error"
skewer judges, and the brief "Unexpounded" attacks the
entire legal profession. He satirizes spelling reformers in
"Orthography" and reformers of any kind in "Incurable."
"Montefiore" combines praise for an individual with a satire
against the human race. The centenarian Sir Moses Haim
Montefiore (1784–1885), who was knighted in 1837 and
made a baronet in 1846, had amassed a fortune on the stock
market. He then retired and became well-known for his in-
ternational philanthropic efforts on behalf of both Jews and
Gentiles.

The preponderance of Bierce's satire, however, was di-
rected against specific figures, like Chauncey Mitchell De-
pew (1834–1928), a New York lawyer, businessman, and rail-
road magnate. An influential Republican, he had turned
down Andrew Johnson's offer of an ambassadorship to Ja-
pan to become president of the New York Central system. In
great demand as an orator and after-dinner speaker, he con-
founded Bierce's prognosis in "A Trencher-Knight" by liv-

ing to the age of ninety-four, remarking, "I get my exercise acting as pallbearer to my friends who exercise." Other targets of Bierce's satire were the Rockefellers in "Compliance," James Whitcomb Riley in "A Literary Method," and George Stoneman (1822–94), California's governor from 1883 to 1887, in "Matter for Gratitude." Bierce was particularly vituperative against judges and lawyers, and his satires of them should be read in the light of his long essay "Some Features of the Law" (*cw* 11:99–129). Although he satirizes Judge Armstrong in "Judex Judicatus" and Judge James McMillan Shafter in "A Growler," his primary target was lawyers: hired mercenaries who bullied helpless witnesses, like George Perry in "To a Bully" and Hall McAllister in "To an Insolent Attorney."

Two of his most noteworthy satires are "Finis Æternitatis" and "A Word to the Unwise." Both combine the cosmic sweep of "The Passing Show" and "A Vision of Doom" with attacks on particular figures. Indeed, "Finis Æternitatis" (which points a finger at Charles Crocker) even uses the same rhyme scheme and stanzaic patterns as "The Passing Show." Bierce criticized Crocker and Collis P. Huntington as "railrogues" who maneuvered legislators into passing bills to further their own commercial interests at the expense of the public weal in what modern economists call "rent-seeking." But it was their colleague "£eland $tanford" (1824–93) who was Bierce's favorite victim. Stanford had been governor of California from 1861 to 1863. In 1885, with the connivance of the Southern Pacific Railroad, he had managed to get himself elected to the U.S. Senate, holding office there to the end of his life; he even aspired to the Presidency. Stanford appears in this anthology in the satirical "Substance or Shadow" and as the subject of one of Bierce's untitled epitaphs. Another epitaph, "Cynic perforce from studying mankind," refers to Frank Morrison Pixley (1825–95), U.S. district attorney under Governor Stanford and President Grant. After a stint as chief editorial writer for the *San Francisco Chronicle,* Pixley became publisher and coeditor of the *Argonaut* (1877–93), for which Bierce wrote from 1877 to 1879. Pixley was a strong supporter of Stanford and the railroad interests; he opposed Oriental immigration and the Catholic church.

Sidney-Fryer characterizes Bierce's satires as "agreeably nasty cast-iron thorns in the Victorian rose-garden" (19). Probably their most significant characteristic is that they embody wit, not humor. Bierce expounded this basic distinction at length in his essay "Wit and Humor" (*cw* 10:98–102), as well as elsewhere. Pitilessly sharp and "as bleak as steel," wit is "a serious matter. To laugh at it is to confess that you do not understand." It "stabs, begs pardon—and turns the weapon in the wound" (quoted in Grenander, *Ambrose Bierce,* 149).

Bierce also makes frequent use of puns in his satire, despite his sallies against them in "The Pun." One is tempted to groan at the last line of "Infralapsarian," but elsewhere in his verses he uses puns with ingenuity and wit: preachers are "birds of pray"; Rockefeller "prays" on his knees—and on his neighbors; and legislators always vote "I." In "Substance or Shadow" the "razor" of a rhetorical trope is a rusty saw. Sometimes Bierce's puns are extremely subtle, as in "Law," where Mercy has "no standing" before the bench because she kneels weeping before it. And Sidney-Fryer (25) has teased a pun out of the title of Bierce's poem "Oneiromancy": "O Near Romance, See." Indeed, Bierce delighted in wordplay of all kinds. In the first line of Salomon's epitaph, his body "reposes"; in the last line, as a patriot he "re-poses."

In Bierce's poetry as a whole, certain features stand out. Although an autodidact, he was a learned man, and the reader who fails to detect the tracks of other writers in his poetry will miss some of its appeal. Sidney-Fryer (28) has indicated "the line of general poetic descent" in Bierce as running from "Edmund Spenser and the Elizabethans to William Blake and the English Romantics," and then to Tennyson, Poe, and Swinburne. More specifically, in Bierce echoes of the Bible and of Shakespeare abound, as do those of Greek and Latin writers, notably in his remarkable translation of "Dies Iræ," a thirteenth-century hymn frequently used in Roman Catholic masses for the dead. Bierce's "Dies Iræ" itself finds an echo in "Matter for Gratitude." Omar Khayyám's *Rubáiyát* in Edward FitzGerald's translation can be traced in some of Bierce's verses; its stanza 82 furnished the title for the collection *Shapes of Clay*.

Bierce parodied Joaquin Miller in "The Mormon Question," a sly hit at Miller's own marital irregularities, and Oliver Goldsmith in "The Perverted Village." Tennyson, Poe, Wordsworth, Coleridge, and Oliver Wendell Holmes, as well as Rabelais, Renan, and Victor Hugo can also be traced in Bierce's poetry. Poe's influence is a rather special one, since it nearly always takes the form of a borrowed metrical pattern and rhyme scheme. But Bierce's attitude toward writers who influenced him was not uncritical adoration. Tennyson's "The Northern Farmer" was dismissed as a mere "thing" (*cw* 10:266) and his "Charge of the Light Brigade" as "resonant patriotic lines" devoid of poetry (10:256–57); Poe's "The Bells" was "rubbishy stuff" (10:257).

As might be expected given his theory of poetry, Bierce

paid a great deal of attention to the arts of versification. In "The Crime of 1903," for example, he effects closure by a subtle change in the pattern of the last verse, and one has only to read a number of his poems to discover the variety and extent of the stanzaic forms he employed. He relied heavily on rhyming iambic pentameter couplets in his satires, but he essayed blank verse in his serious poems and made frequent use of the Petrarchan sonnet in his apostrophes to women. Sidney-Fryer, noting that Bierce is "a master of the run-over line" and that his handling of rhyme, meter, consonance, and assonance "is assured and often ingenious," has called him "an adroit and facile versifier" who is "able to make his poetic statement move through difficult and demanding traditional forms with singular ease" (25).

The poem "Rosalie" may pose a problem in attribution. Was it or was it not written by Bierce? There are arguments on both sides. Negatively, only one point can be raised, but it is an important one. Read with absolute literalness, the poem presents a father speaking to his young daughter. If the narrator is conflated with the author, this situation was obviously impossible for Bierce in December 1869, when "Rosalie" appeared.

But should the poem be read so literally? A very strong indication that "Rosalie" was indeed written by Bierce is the fact that it is signed with the initial *B*, the way he typically identified his early work in periodicals, not only in San Francisco but also in London. Furthermore, a number of other facts should be kept in mind. In "The King of Bores" (157) Bierce states specifically that, "in an idle mood," he pens verses "to nobody, or of her," and that it is pointless to try to identify the addressee. It is, then, certainly within the realm of possibility that "Rosalie" is either a five-finger exercise or a disguised address to Mollie Day, who was a lively and frolicsome young lady. All his life Bierce tended to regard women with an avuncular, paternalistic attitude. Although he was only twenty-seven when "Rosalie" was written, he had been seared by his four years in a bloody war. The battles he survived, and his growing responsibilities as he advanced in rank from private to commissioned officer, can hardly have failed to mature him. And on February 5, 1870, only a little over a month after the publication of "Rosalie," the following note appeared in Bierce's Town Crier column in the *San Francisco News Letter:* "Mollie—tell your mother not to relax her efforts to keep you from writing to us. The chances are that the old lady is right" (Fatout 85).

Finally, the style of "Rosalie" is consistent with its having been written by Bierce. As I have noted, the arts of versification were important to him. Close attention to how they are used in "Rosalie" shows that the three sixteen-line stanzas have both an unusual beat and an unusual rhyme scheme. Lines 1–5, 7, 9, 11, and 13–16 are all trochaic tetrameter catalectic; lines 6, 8, 10, and 12, however (the indented lines), are all true trochaic tetrameter (that is, the unaccented syllable at the end of the last foot is not eliminated). The rhyme scheme is equally artful. The first four lines and the last four lines of each stanza are rhyming couplets. Lines 5–12, however, which include the indented trochaic tetrameter acatalectic lines, all have alternating rhyme (*cdcdefef*). And the last two lines of each stanza all rhyme with each other, ringing changes on "Rosalie."

This pattern bears comparison with that in "Serenade," which is likewise intricate. There the lines scan as trochaic tetrameter catalectic except for the indented lines, which are trochaic trimeter catalectic. The rhyme scheme is *abaaab,* with the second and sixth lines of each stanza all rhyming with each other on the word "do," whose vowel sound is stretched out more and more with each succeeding stanza.

Is "Rosalie" to be regarded, then, as part of the Bierce canon? On the basis of available evidence, the question cannot be closed at this time. Nevertheless, arguments can be adduced that render his authorship at least credible, and I have therefore included the poem in this anthology.

As I hope I have made clear, Bierce's poetic voice was a distinctive one that deserves far more attention than it has received. It was recognized in his own time, however, by at least one fellow poet and critic: Edmund Clarence Stedman. Stedman's *An American Anthology, 1789–1900,* included on pages 443–45 seven poems by Bierce: "The Death of Grant," "The Bride," "Another Way," "Montefiore," "Presentiment," "Creation," and "T. A. H." Stedman chose his entries with tact and taste; I have discussed and cited all of them in this essay.

By and large, however, Bierce's poetry was ignored until the appearance in 1980 of an excellent selection from it, *A Vision of Doom,* edited by Donald Sidney-Fryer. In his thoughtful introductory essay, "A Visionary of Doom," he described Bierce's best poems as "compact, imaginative, and powerful, or—quite unexpectedly—tender" (10). As he observed, they clearly deserve "more attention and appreciation" than they have received to date (29). As I have noted, Bierce's inclusion in the Library of America's new anthology of nineteenth-century verse, as well as in the companion *Garland Encyclopedia,* is an indication that at long last scholars and critics are recognizing his merits not only as a short story writer and witty lexicographer, but also as a poet. The

taste of Bierce's poetry in those books should whet the con-
noisseur's appetite for more. And the selections that follow
this Introduction, it is hoped, will offer the general reader
an opportunity to savor some of the most remarkable verse
in American literary history.

Textual Notes

Except for the *Uncollected Poems* and the instances noted below, the text of the poems in this anthology in every case follows that of Bierce's *Collected Works,* which he carefully revised and proofread himself. Following each poem its source is indicated. The first number indicates the appropriate volume in the *Collected Works,* followed by the page number(s) in that volume. Other (usually earlier) appearances of the poem, where known, follow this entry.

In a letter to his publisher, Walter Neale (Huntington Library MS HM 10384), dated November 28, 1911, Bierce noted errors in "To a Censor" and "Substance or Shadow." Both poems quote the line "Wounds with a touch that's neither felt nor seen." Bierce wanted the words "neither . . . nor" changed to "scarcely . . . or." As the relevant volumes of the *Collected Works* were already in print at the time of Bierce's request, the changes were not made. However, I have emended these two poems in accordance with Bierce's wishes. As he said in his unpublished letter to Neale, "I simply can't help wanting to correct an imperfection where I find it."

In the entries from *The Devil's Dictionary,* I have included only enough of Bierce's definitions to elucidate the verses that follow. The initials "G.J." at the conclusion of a poem refer to "that learned and ingenious cleric, Father Gassalasca Jape, s.j.," an "authority" Bierce often cites in *The Devil's Dictionary,*" along with such other mythical figures as Venable

Strigg, Conmore Apel Brune, Jamrach Holobom, and Sempen Railey.

To avoid ambiguity, in the essays included under "About Poetry" I have silently inserted a comma before the conjunction in a series of three or more items. Bierce customarily did not use a comma in such a place, since these essays appeared originally as journalism, where the practice is looser than that in formal prose.

Bierce divided the essay "Poetry and Verse" into two section, numbering the second, but not the first. The Roman numeral "I" at its beginning is my addition.

Poems from *Collected Works*

TO A DEJECTED POET

Thy gift, if that it be of God,
    Thou hast no warrant to appraise,
    Nor say: "Here part, O Muse, our ways,
The road too stony to be trod."

Not thine to call the labor hard
    And the reward inadequate.
    Who haggles o'er his hire with Fate
Is better bargainer than bard.

What! count the effort labor lost
    When thy good angel holds the reed?
    It were a sorry thing indeed
To stay him till thy palm be crossed.

"The laborer is worthy"—nay,
    The sacred ministry of song
    Is rapture!—'twere a grievous wrong
To fix a wages-rate for play.

Shapes of Clay 4:263.

■

HUMILITY

Great poets fire the world with fagots big
    That make a crackling racket,
But I'm content with but a whispering twig
    To warm some single jacket.

The Scrap Heap 4:368.

GEOTHEOS

As sweet as the look of a lover
    Saluting the eyes of a maid
    That blossom to blue as the maid
Is ablush to the glances above her,
    The sunshine is gilding the glade
    And lifting the lark out of shade.

Sing therefore high praises, and therefore
    Sing songs that are ancient as gold,
    Of earth in her garments of gold;
Nor ask of their meaning, nor wherefore
    They charm as of yore, for behold!
    The Earth is as fair as of old.

Sing songs of the pride of the mountains,
    And songs of the strength of the seas,
    And the fountains that fall to the seas
From the hands of the hills, and the fountains
    That shine in the temples of trees,
    In valleys of roses and bees.

Sing songs that are dreamy and tender,
    Of slender Arabian palms,
    And shadows that circle the palms,
Where caravans out of the splendor
    Are kneeling in blossoms and balms
    In islands of infinite calms.

Barbaric, O Man, was thy runing
    When mountains were stained as with wine
    By the dawning of Time, and as wine
Were the seas, yet its echoes are crooning
    Achant in the gusty pine
    And the pulse of the poet's line.

Shapes of Clay 4:28–29.

■

TEMPORA MUTANTUR

"The world is dull," I cried in my despair:
"Its myths and fables are no longer fair.

"Roll back thy centuries, O Father Time:
To Greece transport me in her golden prime.

"Give back the beautiful old gods again—
The sportive Nymphs, the Dryad's jocund train,

"Pan piping on his reeds, the Naiades,
The Sirens singing by the sleepy seas.

"Nay, show me but a Gorgon and I'll dare
To lift mine eyes to her peculiar hair

"(The fatal horrors of her snaky pate,
That stiffen men into a stony state)

"And die—becoming, as my spirit flies,
A noble statue of myself, life size."

Straight as I spoke I heard the voice of Fate:
"Look up, my lad, the Gorgon sisters wait."

Lifting my eyes, I saw Medusa stand,
Stheno, Euryale, on either hand.

I gazed unpetrified and unappalled—
The girls had aged and were entirely bald!

Shapes of Clay 4:219–20.

■

CREATION

God dreamed—the suns sprang flaming into place,
And sailing worlds with many a venturous race!
He woke—His smile alone illumined space.

The Scrap Heap 4:374; Stedman 444.

THE PASSING SHOW

I

I know not if it was a dream. I viewed
A city where the restless multitude,
    Between the eastern and the western deep
Had reared gigantic fabrics, strong and rude.

Colossal palaces crowned every height;
Towers from valleys climbed into the light;
    O'er dwellings at their feet, great golden domes
Hung in the blue, barbarically bright.

But now, new-glimmering to-east, the day
Touched the black masses with a grace of gray,
    Dim spires of temples to the nation's God
Studding high spaces of the wide survey.

Well did the roofs their solemn secret keep
Of life and death stayed by the truce of sleep,
    Yet whispered of an hour when sleepers wake,
The fool to hope afresh, the wise to weep.

The gardens greened upon the builded hills
Above the tethered thunders of the mills
    With sleeping wheels unstirred to service yet
By the tamed torrents and the quickened rills.

A hewn acclivity, reprieved a space,
Looked on the builder's blocks about his base
    And bared his wounded breast in sign to say:
"Strike! 'tis my destiny to lodge your race.

"'Twas but a breath ago the mammoth browsed
Upon my slopes, and in my caves I housed
    Your shaggy fathers in their nakedness,
While on their foemen's offal they caroused."

Ships from afar afforested the bay.
Within their huge and chambered bodies lay
    The wealth of continents; and merrily sailed
The hardy argosies to far Cathay.

Beside the city of the living spread—
Strange fellowship!—the city of the dead;
    And much I wondered what its humble folk,
To see how bravely they were housed, had said.

Noting how firm their habitations stood,
Broad-based and free of perishable wood—
    How deep in granite and how high in brass
The names were wrought of eminent and good,

I said: "When gold or power is their aim,
The smile of beauty or the wage of shame,
    Men dwell in cities; to this place they fare
When they would conquer an abiding fame."

From the red East the sun—a solemn rite—
Crowned with flame the cross upon a height
    Above the dead; and then with all his strength
Struck the great city all aroar with light!

      II

I know not if it was a dream. I came
Unto a land where something seemed the same
    That I had known as 'twere but yesterday,
But what it was I could not rightly name.

It was a strange and melancholy land,
Silent and desolate. On either hand
　　Lay waters of a sea that seemed as dead,
And dead above it seemed the hills to stand.

Grayed all with age, those lonely hills—ah me,
How worn and weary they appeared to be!
　　Between their feet long dusty fissures clove
The plain in aimless windings to the sea.

One hill there was which, parted from the rest,
Stood where the eastern water curved a-west.
　　Silent and passionless it stood. I thought
I saw a scar upon its giant breast.

The sun with sullen and portentous gleam
Hung like a menace on the sea's extreme;
　　Nor the dead waters, nor the far, bleak bars
Of cloud were conscious of his failing beam.

It was a dismal and a dreadful sight,
That desert in its cold, uncanny light;
　　No soul but I alone to mark the fear
And imminence of everlasting night!

All presages and prophecies of doom
Glimmered and babbled in the ghastly gloom,
　　And in the midst of that accursèd scene
A wolf sat howling on a broken tomb.

Shapes of Clay 4:19–22.

A VISION OF DOOM

I stood upon a hill. The setting sun
Was crimson with a curse and a portent,
And scarce his angry ray lit up the land
That lay below, whose lurid gloom appeared
Freaked with a moving mist, which, reeking up
From dim tarns hateful with some horrid ban,
Took shapes forbidden and without name.
Gigantic night-birds, rising from the reeds
With cries discordant, startled all the air,
And bodiless voices babbled in the gloom—
The ghosts of blasphemies long ages stilled,
And shrieks of women, and men's curses. All
These visible shapes, and sounds no mortal ear
Had ever heard, some spiritual sense
Interpreted, though brokenly; for I
Was haunted by a consciousness of crime,
Some giant guilt, but whose I knew not. All
These things malign, by sight and sound revealed,
Were sin-begotten; that I knew—no more—
And that but dimly, as in dreadful dreams
The sleepy senses babble to the brain
Imperfect witness. As I stood, a voice,
But whence it came I knew not, cried aloud
Some words to me in a forgotten tongue,
Yet straight I knew me for a ghost forlorn,
Returned from the illimited inane.
Again, but in a language that I knew,
As in reply to something which in me
Had shaped itself a thought, but found no words,
It spake from the dread mystery about:

"Immortal shadow of a mortal soul
That perished with eternity, attend.
What thou beholdest is as void as thou:
The shadow of a poet's dream—himself
As thou, his soul as thine, long dead,
But not like thine outlasted by its shade.
His dreams alone survive eternity
As pictures in the unsubstantial void.
Excepting thee and me (and we because
The poet wove us in his thought) remains
Of nature and the universe no part
Nor vestige but the poet's dreams. This dread,
Unspeakable land about thy feet, with all
Its desolation and its terrors—lo!
'Tis but a phantom world. So long ago
That God and all the angels since have died
That poet lived—yourself long dead—his mind
Filled with the light of a prophetic fire,
And standing by the Western sea, above
The youngest, fairest city in the world,
Named in another tongue than his for one
Ensainted, saw its populous domain
Plague-smitten with a nameless shame. For there
Red-handed murder rioted; and there
The people gathered gold, nor cared to loose
The assassin's fingers from the victim's throat,
But said, each in his vile pursuit engrossed:
'Am I my brother's keeper? Let the Law
Look to the matter.' But the Law did not.
And there, O pitiful! The babe was slain
Within its mother's breast and the same grave
Held babe and mother; and the people smiled,

Still gathering gold, and said: 'The Law, the Law.'
Then the great poet, touched upon the lips
With a live coal from Truth's high altar, raised
His arms to heaven and sang a song of doom—
Sang of the time to be, when God should lean
Indignant from the Throne and lift His hand,
And that foul city be no more!—a tale,
A dream, a desolation and a curse!
No vestige of its glory should survive
In fact or memory: its people dead,
Its site forgotten, and its very name
A dream, a desolation and a curse!
No vestige of its glory should survive
In fact or memory: its people dead,
Its site forgotten, and its very name
A dream, a desolation and a curse!
No vestige of its glory should survive
In fact or memory: its people dead,
Its site forgotten, and its very name
Disputed."
        "Was the prophecy fulfilled?"

The sullen disc of the declining sun
Was crimson with a curse and a portent,
And scarce his angry ray lit up the land
Freaked with a moving mist, which, reeking up
From dim tarns hateful with a horrid ban,
Took shapes forbidden and without a name,
And bodiless voices babbled in the gloom.
But not to me came any voice again;
And, covering my face with thin, dead hands,
I wept, and woke, and cried aloud to God!

Black Beetles in Amber 5:46–49.

INVOCATION

Read at the Celebration of Independence in San
          Francisco in 1888.

Goddess of Liberty! O thou
        Whose tearless eyes behold the chain
        And look unmoved upon the slain,
Eternal peace upon thy brow,—

Before thy shrine the races press,
        Thy perfect favor to implore—
        The proudest tyrant asks no more,
The ironed anarchist no less.

Thine altar-coals that touch the lips
        Of prophets kindle, too, the brand
        By Discord flung with wanton hand
Among the houses and the ships.

Upon thy tranquil front the star
        Burns bleak and passionless and white,
        Its cold inclemency of light
More dreadful than the shadows are.

Thy name we do not here invoke
        Our civic rites to sanctify:
        Enthroned in thy remoter sky,
Thou heedest not our broken yoke.

Thou carest not for such as we:
        Our millions die to serve the still
        And secret purpose of thy will.
They perish—what is that to thee?

The light that fills the patriot's tomb
    Is not of thee. The shining crown
    Compassionately offered down
To those who falter in the gloom,

And fall, and call upon thy name,
    And die desiring—'tis the sign
    Of a diviner love than thine,
Rewarding with a richer fame.

To him alone let freemen cry
    Who hears alike the victor's shout,
    The song of faith, the moan of doubt,
And bends him from his nearer sky.

———

God of my country and my race!
    So greater than the gods of old—
    So fairer than the prophets told
Who dimly saw and feared thy face,—

Who didst but half reveal thy will
    And gracious ends to their desire,
    Behind the dawn's advancing fire
Thy tender day-beam veiling still,—

To whom the unceasing suns belong,
    And cause is one with consequence,—
    To whose divine, inclusive sense
The moan is blended with the song,—

Whose laws, imperfect and unjust,
    Thy just and perfect purpose serve:
    The needle, howsoe'er it swerve,
Still warranting the sailor's trust,—

God, lift thy hand and make us free
    To crown the work thou hast designed.
    O, strike away the chains that bind
Our souls to one idolatry!

The liberty thy love hath given
    We thank thee for. We thank thee for
    Our great dead fathers' holy war
Wherein our manacles were riven.

We thank thee for the stronger stroke
    Ourselves delivered and incurred
    When—thine incitement half unheard—
The chains we riveted we broke.

We thank thee that beyond the sea
    Thy people, growing ever wise,
    Turn to the west their serious eyes
And dumbly strive to be as we.

As when the sun's returning flame
    Upon the Nileside statue shone,
    And struck from the enchanted stone
The music of a mighty fame,

Let Man salute the rising day
    Of Liberty, but not adore.
    'Tis Opportunity—no more—
A useful, not a sacred, ray.

It bringeth good, it bringeth ill,
    As he possessing shall elect.
    He maketh it of none effect
Who walketh not within thy will.

Give thou more or less, as we
    Shall serve the right or serve the wrong.
    Confirm our freedom but so long
As we are worthy to be free.

But when (O, distant be the time!)
    Majorities in passion draw
    Insurgent swords to murder Law,
And all the land is red with crime;

Or—nearer menace!—when the band
    Of feeble spirits cringe and plead
    To the gigantic strength of Greed,
And fawn upon his iron hand;—

Nay, when the steps to state are worn
    In hollows by the feet of thieves,
    And Mammon sits among the sheaves
And chuckles while the reapers mourn:

Then stay thy miracle!—replace
    The broken throne, repair the chain,
    Restore the interrupted reign
And veil again thy patient face.

Lo! here upon the world's extreme
    We stand with lifted arms and dare
    By thine eternal name to swear
Our country, which so fair we deem—

Upon whose hills, a bannered throng,
    The spirits of the sun display
    Their flashing lances day by day
And hear the sea's pacific song—

Shall be so ruled in right and grace
    That men shall say: "O, drive afield
    The lawless eagle from the shield,
And call an angel to the place!"

Shapes of Clay 4:34–39. Published in the *San Francisco Examiner,* July 5, 1888; in Ella Sterling Mighels, *The Story of the Files* (San Francisco: World's Fair Commission, 1893); in Mighels, *Literary California* (San Francisco: Harr Wagner, 1918) 187–89; and independently as *An Invocation* (San Francisco: Book Club of California, 1928).

A RATIONAL ANTHEM

My country, 'tis of thee,
Sweet land of felony,
    Of thee I sing—
Land where my fathers fried
Young witches and applied
Whips to the Quaker's hide
    And made him spring.

My knavish country, thee,
Land where the thief is free,
    Thy laws I love;
I love thy thieving bills
That tap the people's tills;
I love thy mob whose will's
    All laws above.

Let Federal employees
And rings rob all they please,
    The whole year long.
Let office-holders make
Their piles and judges rake
Our coin. For Jesus' sake,
    Let's *all* go wrong!

Black Beetles in Amber 5:201; *San
Francisco Wasp,* Sept. 16, 1882.

FREEDOM, *n.*

Exemption from the stress of authority in a beggarly half
dozen of restraint's infinite multitude of methods. A political
condition that every nation supposes itself to enjoy in virtual
monopoly.

Freedom, as every schoolboy knows,
 Once shrieked as Kosciusko fell;
On every wind, indeed, that blows
 I hear her yell.

She screams whenever monarchs meet,
 And parliaments as well,
To bind the chains about her feet
 And toll her knell.

And when the sovereign people cast
 The votes they cannot spell,
Upon the pestilential blast
 Her clamors swell.

For all to whom the power's given
 To sway or to compel,
Among themselves apportion Heaven
 And give her Hell.

   Blary O'Gary.

The Devil's Dictionary 7:107–8.

TO THE BARTHOLDI STATUE

O Liberty, God-gifted—
    Young and immortal maid—
In your high hand uplifted,
    The torch declares your trade.

Its crimson menace, flaming
    Upon the sea and shore,
Is, trumpet-like, proclaiming
    That Law shall be no more.

Austere incendiary,
    We're blinking in the light;
Where is your customary
    Grenade of dynamite?

Where are your staves and switches
    For men of gentle birth?
Your mask and dirk for riches?
    Your chains for wit and worth?

Perhaps, you've brought the halters
    You used in the old days,
When round religion's altars
    You stabled Cromwell's bays?

Behind you, unsuspected,
    Have you the axe, fair wench,
Wherewith you once collected
    A poll-tax from the French?

America salutes you—
    Preparing to "disgorge."
Take everything that suits you,
    And marry Henry George.

1894.

Shapes of Clay 4:153–54.

■

THE HESITATING VETERAN

When I was young and full of faith
    And other fads that youngsters cherish
A cry rose as of one that saith
    With emphasis: "Help or I perish!"
'Twas heard in all the land, and men
    The sound were each to each repeating.
It made my heart beat faster then
    Than any heart can now be beating.

For the world is old and the world is gray—
    Grown prudent and, I think, more witty.
She's cut her wisdom teeth, they say,
    And doesn't now go in for Pity.
Besides, the melancholy cry
    Was that of one, 'tis now conceded,
Whose plight no one beneath the sky
    Felt half so poignantly as he did.

Moreover, he was black. And yet
    That sentimental generation

With an austere compassion set
    Its face and faith to the occasion.
Then there were hate and strife to spare,
    And various hard knocks a-plenty;
And I ('twas more than my true share,
    I must confess) took five-and-twenty.

That all is over now—the reign
    Of love and trade stills all dissensions,
And the clear heavens arch again
    Above a land of peace and pensions.
The black chap—at the last we gave
    Him everything that he had cried for,
Though many white chaps in the grave
    'Twould puzzle to say what they died for.

I hope he's better off—I trust
    That his society and his master's
Are worth the price we paid, and must
    Continue paying, in disasters;
But sometimes doubts press thronging round
    ('Tis mostly when my hurts are aching)
If war for Union was a sound
    And profitable undertaking.

'Tis said they mean to take away
    The Negro's vote for he's unlettered.
'Tis true he sits in darkness day
    And night, as formerly, when fettered;
But pray observe—howe'er he vote
    To whatsoever party turning,
He'll be with gentlemen of note
    And wealth and consequence and learning.

With saints and sages on each side,
   How could a fool through lack of knowledge,
Vote wrong? If learning is no guide
   Why ought one to have been in college?
O Son of Day, O Son of Night!
   What are your preferences made of?
I know not which of you is right,
   Nor which to be the more afraid of.

The world is old and the world is bad,
   And creaks and grinds upon its axis;
And man's an ape and the gods are mad!—
   There's nothing sure, not even our taxes.
No mortal man can Truth restore,
   Or say where she is to be sought for.
I know what uniform I wore—
   O, that I knew which side I fought for!

Shapes of Clay 4:115–18.

A YEAR'S "CASUALTIES"

Slain as they lay by the secret, slow,
Pitiless hand of an unseen foe,
Two score thousand old soldiers have crossed
The river to join the loved and lost.
In the space of a year their spirits fled,
Silent and white, to the camp of the dead.

One after one they fall asleep
And the pension agents awake to weep,
And orphaned statesmen are loud in their wail
As the souls flit by on the evening gale.
O Father of Battles, pray give us release
From the horrors of peace, the horrors of peace!

Shapes of Clay 4:118.

■

AT A "NATIONAL ENCAMPMENT"

You're grayer than one would have thought you:
    The climate you have over there
In the East has apparently brought you
    Disorders affecting the hair,
    Which—pardon me—seems a bit spare.

You'll not take offence at my giving
    Expression to notions like these.
You might have been stronger if living
    Out here in our sanative breeze.
    It's unhealthy here for disease.

No, I'm not so plump as a pullet,
    But that's the old wound, you see.

Remember my paunching a bullet?—
    And how that it didn't agree
    With?—well, honest hardtack for me.

Just pass me the wine—I've a helly
    And horrible kind of drouth!
When a fellow has that in his belly
    Which didn't go in at his mouth
    He's hotter than all Down South!

Great Scott! what a nasty day *that* was—
    When every galoot in our crack
Division who didn't lie flat was
    Dissuaded from further attack
    By the bullet's felicitous whack.

'Twas there that our major slept under
    Some cannon of ours on the crest,
Till they woke him by stilling their thunder,
    And he cursed them for breaking his rest,
    And died in the midst of his jest.

That night—it was late in November—
    The dead seemed uncommonly chill
To the touch; and a chap I remember
    Who took it exceedingly ill
    When I dragged myself over his bill.

Well, comrades, I'm off now—good morning.
    Your talk is as pleasant as pie,
But, pardon me, one word of warning:
    Speak little and seldom, say I.
    That's my way. God bless you. Good-bye.

Black Beetles in Amber 5:40–42; *San Francisco
Wasp,* July 31, 1886.

THE CONFEDERATE FLAGS

Tut-tut! give back the flags—how can you care,
  You veterans and heroes?
Why should you at a kind intention swear
  Like twenty Neros?

Suppose the act was not so overwise—
  Suppose it was illegal;
Is't well on such a question to arise
  And pinch the Eagle?

Nay, let's economize his breath to scold
  And terrify the alien
Who tackles him, as Hercules of old
  The bird Stymphalian.

Among the rebels when we made a breach
  Was it to get their banners?
That was but incidental—'twas to teach
  Them better manners.

They know the lesson well enough to-day;
  Now, let us try to show them
That we're not only stronger far than they,
  (How we did mow them!)

But more magnanimous. My lads, 'tis plain
  'Twas an uncommon riot;
The warlike tribes of Europe fight for gain;
  We fought for quiet.

If we were victors, then we all must live
  With the same flag above us;

'Twas all in vain unless we now forgive
    And make them love us.

Let kings keep trophies to display above
    Their doors like any savage;
The freeman's trophy is the foeman's love,
    Despite war's ravage.

"Make treason odious?" My friends, you'll find
    You can't, in right and reason,
While "Washington" and "treason" are combined—
    "Hugo" and " treason."

All human governments must take the chance
    And hazard of sedition.
O wretch! to pledge your manhood in advance
    To blind submission.

It may be wrong, it may be right, to rise
    In warlike insurrection:
The loyalty that fools so dearly prize
    May mean subjection.

Be loyal to your country, yes—but how
    If tyrants hold dominion?
The South believed they did; can't you allow
    For that opinion?

He who will never rise though rulers plot,
    His liberties despising—
How is he manlier than the *sans-culottes*
    Who's always rising?

Give back the foolish flags whose bearers fell,
>   Too valiant to forsake them.
Is it presumptuous, this counsel? Well,
>   I helped to take them.

1891.

Shapes of Clay 4:335–37.

■

TO E. S. SALOMON,

Who in a Memorial Day oration protested bitterly
against decorating the graves of Confederate dead.

What! Salomon! such words from you,
>   Who call yourself a soldier? Well,
>   The Southern brother where he fell
Slept all your base oration through.

Alike to him—he cannot know
>   Your praise or blame: as little harm
>   Your tongue can do him as your arm
A quarter-century ago.

The brave respect the brave. The brave
>   Respect the dead; but *you*—you draw
>   That ancient blade, the ass's jaw,
And shake it o'er a hero's grave.

Are you not he who makes to-day
>   A merchandise of old renown
>   Which he persuades this easy town
He won in battle far away?

Nay, those the fallen who revile
    Have ne'er before the living stood
    And stoutly made their battle good
And greeted danger with a smile.

What if the dead whom still you hate
    Were wrong? Are you so surely right?
    We know the issues of the fight—
The sword is but an advocate.

Men live and die, and other men
    Arise with knowledges diverse:
    What seemed a blessing seems a curse,
And Now is still at odds with Then.

The years go on, the old comes back
    To mock the new—beneath the sun
    Is *nothing* new; ideas run
Recurrent in an endless track.

What most we censure, men as wise
    Have reverently practised; nor
    Will future wisdom fail to war
On principles we dearly prize.

We do not know—we can but deem,
    And he is loyalest and best
    Who takes the light full on his breast
And follows it throughout the dream.

The broken light, the shadows wide—
    Behold the battle-field displayed!
    God save the vanquished from the blade,
The victor from the victor's pride!

If, Salomon, the blessed dew
      That falls upon the Blue and Gray
      Is powerless to wash away
The sin of differing from you,

Remember how the flood of years
      Has rolled across the erring slain;
      Remember, too, the cleansing rain
Of widows' and of orphans' tears.

The dead are dead—let that atone:
      And though with equal hand we strew
      The blooms on saint and sinner too,
Yet God will know to choose his own.

The wretch, whate'er his life and lot,
      Who does not love the harmless dead
      With all his heart and all his head—
May God forgive him, *I* shall not.

When, Salomon, you come to quaff
      The Darker Cup with meeker face,
      I, loving you at last, shall trace
Upon your tomb this epitaph:

"Draw near, ye generous and brave—
      Kneel round this monument and weep
      For one who tried in vain to keep
A flower from a soldier's grave."

Black Beetles in Amber 5:62–64.

THE DEATH OF GRANT

Father! whose hard and cruel law
    Is part of thy compassion's plan,
    Thy works presumptuously we scan
For what the prophets say they saw.

Unbidden still the awful slope
    Walling us in we climb to gain
    Assurance of the shining plain
That faith has certified to hope.

In vain!—beyond the circling hill
    The shadow and the cloud abide.
    Subdue the doubt, our spirits guide
To trust the record and be still.

To trust it loyally as he
    Who, heedful of his high design,
    Ne'er raised a seeking eye to thine,
But wrought thy will unconsciously,

Disputing not of chance or fate,
    Nor questioning of cause or creed;
    For anything but duty's deed
Too simply wise, too humbly great.

The cannon syllabled his name;
    His shadow shifted o'er the land,
    Portentous, as at his demand
Successive bastions sprang to flame!

He flared the continent with fire,
    The rivers ran in lines of light!

Thy will be done on earth—if right
Or wrong he cared not to inquire.

His was the heavy hand, and his
     The service of the despot blade;
     His the soft answer that allayed
War's giant animosities.

Let us have peace: our clouded eyes,
     Fill, Father, with another light,
     That we may see with clearer sight
Thy servant's soul in Paradise.

Shapes of Clay 4:131–32; *San Francisco
Wasp* August 1, 1885; Stedman 443.

■

CONTENTMENT

Sleep fell upon my senses and I dreamed
     Long years had circled since my life had fled.
The world was different, and all things seemed
     Remote and strange, like noises to the dead.
     And one great Voice there was; and some one said:
"Posterity is speaking—rightly deemed
Infallible"; and so I gave attention,
Hoping Posterity my name would mention.

"Illustrious Spirit," said the Voice, "appear!
     While we confirm eternally thy fame,
Before our dread tribunal answer, here,
     Why do no statues celebrate thy name,
     No monuments thy services proclaim?

Why did not thy contemporaries rear
To thee some schoolhouse or memorial college?
It looks almighty queer, you must acknowledge."

Up spake I hotly: "That is where you err!"
      But some one thundered in my ear: "You shan't
Be interrupting these proceedings, sir;
      The question was addressed to General Grant."
      Some other things were spoken which I can't
Distinctly now recall, but I infer,
By certain flushings of my cheek and forehead,
Posterity's environment is torrid.

Then heard I (this was in a dream, remark)
      Another Voice, clear, comfortable, strong,
As Grant's great shade, replying from the dark,
      Said in a tone that rang the earth along,
      And thrilled the senses of the judges' throng:
"I'd rather you would question why, in park
And street, my monuments were not erected
Than why they were." Then, waking, I reflected.

1885.

Shapes of Clay 4:221–22.

ONEIROMANCY

I fell asleep and dreamed that I
Was flung, like Vulcan, from the sky;
Like him, was lamed—another part:
His leg was crippled, and my heart.
I woke in time to see my love
Conceal a letter in her glove.

The Scrap Heap 4:363.

■

NOVUM ORGANUM

In Bacon see the culminating prime
Of British intellect and British crime.
He died, and Nature, settling his affairs,
Parted his powers among us, his heirs:
To each a pinch of common-sense, for seed,
And, to develop it, a pinch of greed.
Each frugal heir, to make the gift suffice,
Buries the talent to manure the vice.

Bits of Autobiography 1:356; *The
Lantern* (London), May 18, 1874.

A VOICE FROM PEKIN

"'Empress of China'! I nor rule nor reign:
I wear the purple but to hide the chain—
Free only to hold back the open door
For foreign devils drunk upon my floor."

The Scrap Heap 4:369.

■

FRANCE

Unhappy State! with horrors still to strive:
Thy Hugo dead, thy Boulanger alive;
A Prince who'd govern where he dares not dwell,
And who for power would his birthright sell—
Who, eager o'er his enemies to reign,
Grabs at the scepter and conceals the chain;
While pugnant factions mutually strive
By cutting throats to keep the land alive.
Perverse in passion, as in pride perverse—
To all a mistress, to thyself a curse;
Sweetheart of Europe! every sun's embrace
Matures the charm and poison of thy grace.
Yet time to thee nor peace nor wisdom brings;
In blood of citizens and blood of kings
The stones of thy stability are set,
And the fair fabric trembles at a threat.

Shapes of Clay 4:309.

A FALSE PROPHECY

Dom Pedro, Emperor of far Brazil
    (Whence coffee comes, and the three-cornered nut)
They say that you're imperially ill,
    And threatened with paralysis. Tut-tut!
    Though Emperors are mortal, nothing but
A nimble thunderbolt could catch and kill
A man predestined to depart this life
By the assassin's bullet, bomb or knife.

Sir, once there was a President who freed
    Four million slaves; and once there was a Czar
Who freed ten times as many serfs. Sins breed
    The means of punishment, and tyrants are
    Hurled headlong out of the triumphal car
If faster than the law allows they speed.
Lincoln and Alexander struck a rut;
You freed slaves too. Paralysis!—tut-tut.

1885.

Shapes of Clay 4:311.

■

THE EASTERN QUESTION

Looking across the line, the Grecian said:
"This border I will stain a Turkey red."
The Moslem smiled serenely and replied:
"No Greek has ever for his country dyed."
While thus each patriot guarded his frontier
The Powers stole the country in his rear.

The Scrap Heap 4:367.

THE CRIME OF 1903

Time was, not very long ago,
    As by historians time is reckoned,
When first of virtues here below
Was hatred of secession, though
    Some swore it wasn't even second;
But these (they mostly were down South)
    Have all renounced their view with candor—
Some tardily by word of mouth,
    Some, earlier, in a manner grander.

To stamp their error out,'tis true,
    We paid enough of blood (the treasure
Would pave with gold an avenue)
To float a battleship or two,
    If so the cost we choose to measure.
'Twas worth it all, we say and say,—
    The President has often said it;
And so it was, to *us;* and they
    Say nothing, as a rule, who shed it.

"Times change and we change with them," men
    Of old renown averred in Latin;
And that's as true on tongue or pen
This blessed century as when
    The seat of empire Cæsar sat in.
For see how many play their parts
    As ardent lovers of secession,
Promoting it with all their hearts—
    In countries out of our possession.

O men of variable views,
    How can you be so light and fickle?

Is it because you think the news
From Panama portends no bruise
    To you, nor payment of a nickel?
Nay, is it that you scent a gain
    In troubles of a neighbor nation,
And so appraise her loss and pain
    As nothing worth a valuation?

Those ills 'tis easy to endure
    That light upon and sting another—
That's Christian fortitude; but sure
There's somewhere an account of your
    Least feeling toward a hapless brother.
Himself may show by deed and speech
    Less racial sympathies than tribal,
But—well, this is no place to preach;
    The sermon's mostly in the Bible.

We're false to trust and quick to spy
    The fissure in a friendly armor,
Even Freedom can no more rely
    Upon our promise not to harm her.
O Guardian of Continents,
    My country! shall that evil dower,
The passion for preëminence,
Cry from thy seaward battlements
    A soul already drunk with power?

1903.

Shapes of Clay 4:146–48.

SAITH THE CZAR

My people come to me and make their moan:
"We starve, your Majesty—give us a stone."
That's flat rebellion!—how the devil dare
They starve right in my capital? Their prayer
For something in their bellies I will meet
With that which I'll not trouble them to eat.
They ask for greater freedom. No, indeed—
What happened to my ancestor who freed
The serfs? His grateful subjects duly flung
Something that spoke to him without a tongue.
So he was sacrificed for Freedom's sake,
And gathered to his fathers with a rake.
I from Autocracy my people free?
Ah, would to Heaven they could deliver me!

Shapes of Clay 4:208.

■

AFTER PORTSMOUTH

Begirt with bombs that fall and flames that rise,
The Tsar, bewildered, stares. "Alas," he cries,
"Life withholds joy and death denies release!
And Roosevelt would have me think this peace."

The Scrap Heap 4:369.

A FAIR DIVISION

Another Irish landlord gone to grass,
Slain by the bullets of the tenant class!
Pray, good agrarians, what wrong requires
Such foul redress? Between you and the squires
All Ireland's parted with an even hand—
For you have all the ire, they all the land.

The Scrap Heap 4:360.

■

STRAINED RELATIONS

Says England to Germany: "Africa's ours."
    Says Germany: "Ours, I opine."
Says Africa: "Tell me, delectable Powers,
    What is it that ought to be mine?"

The Scrap Heap 4:368.

■

A LACKING FACTOR

"You acted unwisely," I cried, "as you see
    By the outcome." He calmly eyed me:
"When choosing the course of my action," said he,
    "I had not the outcome to guide me."

The Scrap Heap 4:360.

TWO TYPES

Courageous fool—the peril's strength unknown.
Courageous man!—so conscious of your own.

The Scrap Heap 4:367.

■

ELEGY, *n*.

A composition in verse, in which, without employing any of the
methods of humor, the writer aims to produce in the reader's
mind the dampest kind of dejection. The most famous English
example begins somewhat like this:

The cur foretells the knell of parting day;
    The loafing herd winds slowly o'er the lea;
The wise man homeward plods; I only stay
    To fiddle-faddle in a minor key.

The Devil's Dictionary 7:83.

■

IN MEMORIAM

Beauty (they called her) wasn't a maid
Of many things in the world afraid.
She wasn't a maid who turned and fled
At sight of a mouse, alive or dead.
She wasn't a maid a man could "shoo"
By shouting, however abruptly, "Boo!"
She wasn't a maid who'd run and hide
If her face and figure you idly eyed.

She wasn't a maid who'd blush and shake
When asked what part of the fowl she'd take.
(I blush myself to confess she preferred,
And commonly got, the most of the bird.)
She wasn't a maid to simper because
She was asked to sing—if she ever was.
In short, if the truth must be displayed
All naked—Beauty wasn't a maid.

Beauty, furry and fine and fat,
Yawny and clawy, sleek and all that,
Was a pampered and spoiled Angora cat!
I loved her well, and I'm proud that she
Wasn't indifferent, quite, to me;
In fact I have sometimes gone so far
(You know, mesdames, how silly men are)
As to think she preferred—excuse the conceit—
My legs upon which to sharpen her feet.
Perhaps it shouldn't have counted for much,
But I started and thrilled beneath her touch!

Ah, well, that's ancient history now:
The fingers of Time have touched my brow,
And I hear with never a start to-day
That Beauty has passed from the earth away.
Gone!—her death-song (it killed her) sung.
Gone!—her fiddlestrings all unstrung.
Gone to the bliss of a new *régime*
Of turkey smothered in seas of cream;
Of roasted mice (a superior breed,
To science unknown and the coarser need
Of the living cat) cooked by the flame
Of the dainty soul of an erring dame

Who had given to purity all her care,
Neglecting the duty of daily prayer,—
Crisp, delicate mice, just touched with spice
By the ghost of a breeze from Paradise;
A very digestible sort of mice.

Let scoffers sneer, I purpose to hold
That Beauty has mounted the Stair of Gold,
To eat and eat, forever and aye,
On a velvet rug from a golden tray.
But the human spirit—that is my creed—
Rots in the ground like a barren seed.
That is my creed, abhorred by Man
But approved by Cat since time began.
Till Death shall kick at me, thundering "Scat!"
I shall hold to that, I shall hold to that.

Shapes of Clay 4:163–65.

■

CALIFORNIAN SUMMER PICTURES

To the Happy Hunting Grounds

Wide windy reaches of high stubble field;
A long gray road, bordered with dusty pines;
A wagon moving in a "cloud by day";
Two city sportsmen with a dove between,
Breast-high upon a fence and fast asleep—
A solitary dove, the only dove
In twenty counties, and it sick, or else
It were not there. Two guns that fire as one,

With thunder simultaneous and loud;
Two shattered human wrecks of blood and bone!
And later, in the gloaming, comes a man—
The worthy local coroner is he,
Renowned all thereabout, and popular
With many a remain. All tenderly
Compiling in a game-bag the remains,
He glides into the gloom and fades from sight.
The dove, cured of its ailment by the shock,
Has flown, meantime, on pinions strong and fleet,
To die of age in some far foreign land.

Black Beetles in Amber 5:277–78.

■

THE GOLDEN AGE

Long ago the world was finer—
    Why it failed I do not know:
All the virtues were diviner;
Robber, miser, and maligner
        Had not been created. No,
        Truth and honor flourished, though,
            Long ago.

Sages in procession stalking
    Moved majestic to and fro,
And each lowly mortal walking
In their shadow stilled his talking,
        Heeding the sonorous flow
        Of their wisdom, loud or low,
            Long ago.

Angel Woman, younger, fairer
    Far than she that now we know,
Gave men meeting with a rarer
Grace. No graybeard cried, "Beware her
    Tongue and temper!" She was slow
    To wrath. I tell you that was so,
        Long ago.

Ah, the miracle of morning,
    Setting all the world aglow
Like a smile of light adorning
God's own face, held no forewarning
    Of the tempest that would blow—
    Sign and prophecy of woe,
        Long ago.

Hope from every hilltop beckoned
    To the happy throngs below;
And they confidently reckoned
On a hero every second.
    Best of all that goodly show,
    I was but a laddie—O,
        So long ago!

Shapes of Clay 4:90–92.

MACROBIAN, *n*.

One forgotten of the gods and living to a great
age. . . . The verses following were written by a
macrobian:

When I was young the world was fair
    And amiable and sunny.
A brightness was in all the air,
    In all the waters, honey.
    The jokes were fine and funny,
The statesmen honest in their views,
    And in their lives, as well,
And when you heard a bit of news
    'Twas true enough to tell.
Men were not ranting, shouting, reeking,
Nor women "generally speaking."

The Summer then was long indeed:
    It lasted one whole season!
The sparkling Winter gave no heed
    When ordered by Unreason
    To bring the early peas on.
Now, where the dickens is the sense
    In calling that a year
Which does no more than just commence
    Before the end is near?
When I was young the year extended
From month to month until it ended.

I know not why the world has changed
    To something dark and dreary,
And everything is now arranged
    To make a fellow weary.

The Weather Man—I fear he
Has much to do with it, for, sure,
    The air is not the same:
It chokes you when it is impure,
    When pure it makes you lame.
With windows closed you are asthmatic;
Open, neuralgic or sciatic.

Well, I suppose this new régime
    Of dun degeneration
Seems eviler than it would seem
    To a better observation,
    And has for compensation
Some blessings in a deep disguise
    Which mortal sight has failed
To pierce, although to angels' eyes
    They're visibly unveiled.
If Age is such a boon, good land!
He's costumed by a master hand!

Venable Strigg.

The Devil's Dictionary 7:204–6.

A STUDY IN GRAY

I step from the door with a shiver
    (This fog is uncommonly cold)
And ask myself: What did I give her?—
      The maiden a trifle gone-old,
      With the head of gray hair that was gold.

Ah, well, I suppose 'twas a dollar,
    And doubtless the change is correct,
Though it's odd that it seems so much smaller
      Than what I'd a right to expect.
      But you pay when you dine, I reflect.

So I walk up the street—'twas a saunter
    A score of years back, when I strolled
From this door; and our talk was all banter
      Those days when her hair was of gold,
      And the sea-fog less searching and cold.

A score? Why, that isn't so very
    Much time to have lost from a life.
There's reason enough to be merry:
      I've not fallen down in the strife,
      But marched with the drum and the fife.

If Hope, when she lured me and beckoned,
    Had pushed at my shoulders instead,
And Fame, on whose favors I reckoned,
      Had laureled the worthiest head,
      I could hallow the years that are dead.

Believe me, I've held my own, mostly
    Through all of this wild masquerade;

But somehow the fog is more ghostly
    To-night, and the skies are more grayed,
    Like the locks of the restaurant maid.

If ever I'd fainted and faltered
    I'd fancy this did but appear;
But the climate, I'm certain, has altered—
    Grown colder and more austere
    Than it was in that earlier year.

The lights, too, are strangely unsteady
    That lead from the street to the quay.
I think they'll go out—and I'm ready
    To follow. Out there in the sea
    The fog-bell is calling to me.

Shapes of Clay 4:259–60.

■

A GUEST

Death, are you well? I trust you have no cough
    That's painful or in any way annoying—
No kidney trouble that may carry you off,
    Nor heart disease to keep you from enjoying
Your meals—and ours. 'Twere very sad indeed
To have to quit the busy life you lead.

You've been quite active lately for so old
    A person, and not very strong-appearing.
I'm apprehensive, somehow, that my bold,
    Bad brother gave you trouble in the spearing.

And my two friends—I fear, sir, that you ran
Quite hard for them, especially the man.

I crave your pardon: 'twas no fault of mine;
    If you are overworked I'm sorry, very.
Come in, old man, and have a glass of wine.
        What shall it be—madeira, port or sherry?
What! just a mug of blood? That's funny grog
To ask a friend for, eh? Well, take it, hog!

Shapes of Clay 4:310.

■

WILLIAM F. SMITH

Light lie the earth upon his dear dead heart,
    And dreams disturb him never.
Be deeper peace than Paradise his part
    Forever and forever.

Black Beetles in Amber 5:306.

ANOTHER WAY

I lay in silence, dead. A woman came
       And laid a rose upon my breast and said:
"May God be merciful." She spoke my name,
       And added: "It is strange to think him dead.

"He loved me well enough, but 'twas his way
       To speak it lightly." Then, beneath her breath:
"Besides"—I knew what further she would say,
       But then a footfall broke my dream of death.

To-day the words are mine. I lay the rose
       Upon her breast, and speak her name, and deem
It strange indeed that she is dead. God knows
       I had more pleasure in the other dream.

Shapes of Clay 4:193; Stedman 444.

■

PRESENTIMENT

With saintly grace and reverent tread,
       She walked among the graves with me;
       Her every foot-fall seemed to be
A benediction on the dead.

The guardian spirit of the place
       She seemed, and I some ghost forlorn
       Surprised in the untimely morn
She made with her resplendent face.

Moved by some waywardness of will,
       Three paces from the path apart

She stepped and stood—my prescient heart
Was stricken with a passing chill.

The folk-lore of the years agone
        Remembering, I smiled and thought:
        "Who shudders suddenly at naught,
His grave is being trod upon."

But now I know that it was more
        Than idle fancy. O, my sweet,
        I did not think so little feet
Could make a buried heart so sore!

Shapes of Clay 4:258; Stedman 444.

■

J. F. B.

How well this man unfolded to our view
        The world's beliefs of Death and Heaven and Hell—
        This man whose own convictions none could tell,
Nor if his maze of reason had a clew.
Dogmas he wrote for daily bread, but knew
        The fair philosophies of doubt so well
        That while we listened to his words there fell
Some that were strangely cornforting if true.
Marking how wise we grew upon his doubt,
        We said: "If so, by groping in the night,
        He can proclaim some certain paths of trust,
How great our profit if he saw about
        His feet the highways leading to the light."
        Now he sees all. Ah, Christ! his mouth is dust!

Shapes of Clay 4:129; *San Francisco Wasp,* May 5, 1882.

T. A. H.

Yes, he was that, or that, as you prefer—
Did so and so, though, faith, it wasn't all;
Lived like a fool, or a philosopher,
And had whatever's needful to a fall.
As rough inflections on a planet merge
In the true bend of the gigantic sphere,
Nor mar the perfect circle of its verge,
So in the survey of his worth the small
Asperities of spirit disappear,
Lost in the grander curves of character.
He lately was hit hard; none knew but I
The strength and terror of that ghastly stroke—
Not even herself. He uttered not a cry,
But set his teeth and made a revelry;
Drank like a devil—straining sometimes red
The goblet's edge; diced with his conscience; spread,
Like Sisyphus, a feast for Death and spoke
His welcome in a tongue so long forgot
That even his ancient guest remembered not
What race had cursed him in it. Thus my friend,
Still conjugating with each failing sense
The verb "to die" in every mood and tense,
Pursued his awful humor to the end.
When like a stormy dawn the crimson broke
From his white lips he smiled and mutely bled,
And, having meanly lived, is grandly dead.

Shapes of Clay 4:67; Stedman 444–45.

REMINDED

Beneath my window twilight made
Familiar mysteries of shade.
Faint voices from the darkening down
Were calling vaguely to the town.

Intent upon a low, far gleam
That burned upon the world's extreme,
I sat, with short reprieve from grief,
And turned the volume, leaf by leaf,
Wherein a hand long dead had wrought
A million miracles of thought.
My fingers carelessly unclung
The lettered pages, and among
Them wandered witless, nor divined
The wealth in which, poor fools, they mined.
The soul that should have led their quest
Was dreaming in the level west,
Where a tall tower, stark and still,
Uplifted on a distant hill,
Stood lone and passionless to claim
Its guardian star's returning flame.

I know not how my dream was broke,
But suddenly my spirit woke
Filled with a foolish fear to look
Upon the hand that clove the book,
Significantly pointing; next
I bent attentive to the text,
And read—and as I read grew old—
The mindless words: "Poor Tom's a-cold!"

Ah me! to what a subtle touch

The brimming cup resigns its clutch
Upon the wine. Dear God, is't writ
That hearts their overburden bear
Of bitterness though thou permit
The pranks of Chance, alurk in nooks,
And striking coward blows from books,
And dead hands reaching everywhere?

Shapes of Clay 4:189–90.

■

TO A CENSOR

The delay granted by the weakness and good nature
of our judges is responsible for half the murders.
—*Daily Newspaper.*

Delay responsible? Why, then, my friend,
Impeach Delay and you will make an end.
Thrust vile Delay in jail and let it rot
For doing all the things that it should not.
Put not good-natured judges under bond,
But make Delay in damages respond.
Minos, Æacus, Rhadamanthus, rolled
Into one pitiless, unsmiling scold—
Unsparing censor, be your thongs uncurled
To "lash the rascals naked through the world."
The rascals? Nay, Rascality's the thing
Above whose back your knotted scourges sing.
Your satire, truly, like a razor keen,
"Wounds with a touch that's scarcely felt or seen";
For naught that you assail with falchion free
Has either nerves to feel or eyes to see.

Against abstractions evermore you charge:
You hack no helmet and you need no targe.

That wickedness is wrong and sin a vice,
That wrong's not right, nor foulness ever nice,
Fearless affirm. All consequences dare:
Smite the offense and the offender spare.
When Ananias and Sapphira lied
Falsehood, had you been there, had surely died.
When money-changers in the Temple sat,
At money-changing you'd have whirled the "cat"
(That John-the-Baptist of the modern pen)
And all those brokers would have cried amen!

Good friend, if any judge deserve your blame
Have you no courage, or has he no name?
Upon his method will you wreak your wrath,
Himself all unmolested in his path?
Fall to! fall to!—your club no longer draw
To beat the air or flail a man of straw.
Scorn to do justice like the Saxon thrall
Who cuffed the offender's shadow on a wall.
Let rascals in the flesh attest your zeal—
Knocked on the mazzard or tripped up at heel!

We know that judges are corrupt. We know
That crimes are lively and that laws are slow.
We know that lawyers lie and doctors slay;
That priests and preachers are but birds of pray;
That merchants cheat and journalists for gold
Flatter the vicious while at vice they scold.
'Tis all familiar as the simple lore
That two policemen and two thieves make four.

But since, while some are wicked some are good
(As trees may differ though they all are wood)
Names here and there, to show whose head is hit,
The bad would sentence and the good acquit.
In sparing everybody none you spare:
Rebukes most personal are least unfair.
To fire at random if you still prefer,
And swear at Dog but never kick a cur,
Permit me yet one ultimate appeal
To something that you understand and feel:
Let thrift and vanity your heart persuade—
You might be read if you would learn your trade.

Good brother censors (you have doubtless guessed
Not one of you but all are here addressed)
Remember this: the shaft that seeks a heart
Draws all eyes after it; an idle dart
Shot at some shadow flutters o'er the green,
Its flight unheeded and its fall unseen.

Shapes of Clay 4:110–12.

■

SUBSTANCE OR SHADOW

So, gentle critics, you would have me tilt,
Not at the guilty, only at their guilt!—
Spare the offender and condemn Offense,
And make life miserable to Pretense!
"Whip Vice and Folly—that is satire's use—
But be not personal, for *that's* abuse;
Nor e'er forget what, 'like a razor keen,

Wounds with a touch that's scarcely felt or seen.' "
Well, friends, I venture, destitute of awe,
To think that razor but an old, old saw,
A trifle rusty; and a wound, I'm sure,
That's felt not, seen not, one can well endure.
Go to! go to!—you're as unfitted quite
To give advice to writers as to write.
I find in Folly and in Vice a lack
Of head to strike, and for the lash no back,
Whilst Pixley has a pow that's easy struck.
And though good Deacon Fitch (a Fitch for luck!)
Has none, yet, lest he go entirely free,
God gave to him a corn, a heel to me.
He, also, sets his face (so like a flint
The wonder grows that Pickering doesn't skin't)
With cold austerity, against these wars
On scamps—'tis Scampery that *he* abhors!

Behold advances in dignity and state—
Grave, smug, serene, indubitably great—
Stanford, philanthropist! One hand bestows
In alms what t'other one to justice owes.
Rascality attends him like a shade,
But closes, woundless, o'er my baffled blade,
Its limbs unsevered, spirit undismayed.
Faith! I'm for something can be made to feel,
If, like Pelides, only in the heel.
The fellow's self invites assault; his crimes
Will each bear killing twenty thousand times!
Anon Creed Haymond—but the list is long
Of names to point the moral of my song.
Rogues, fools, impostors, sycophants, they rise;

They foul the earth and horrify the skies—
With Collis Huntington (sole honest man
In all the reek of that rapscallion clan)
Denouncing Theft as hard as e'er he can!

Black Beetles in Amber 5:248–50.

■

THE STATESMEN

How blest the land that counts among
    Her sons so many good and wise,
To execute great feats of tongue
    When troubles rise.

Behold them mounting every stump,
    By speech our liberty to guard.
Observe their courage—see them jump,
    And come down hard!

"Walk up, walk up!" each cries aloud,
    "And learn from me what you must do
To turn aside the thunder cloud,
    The earthquake too.

"Beware the wiles of yonder quack
    Who stuffs the ears of all that pass.
I—I alone can show that black
    Is white as grass."

They shout through all the day and break
    The silence of the night as well.
They'd make—I wish they'd *go* and make—
    Of Heaven a Hell.

A advocates free silver, B
      Free trade and C free banking laws.
Free board, clothes, lodging would from me
      Win warm applause.

Lo, D lifts up his voice: "You see
      The single tax on land would fall
On all alike." More evenly
      No tax at all.

"With paper money," bellows E,
      "We'll all be rich as lords." No doubt—
And richest of the lot will be
      The chap without.

As many "cures" as addle-wits
      Who know not what the ailment is!
Meanwhile the patient foams and spits
      Like a gin-fizz.

Alas, poor Body Politic,
      Your fate is all too clearly read:
To be not altogether quick,
      Nor very dead.

You take your exercise in squirms,
      Your rest in fainting fits between.
'Tis plain that your disorder's worms—
      Worms fat and lean.

Worm Capital, Worm Labor dwell
      Within your maw and muscle's scope.
Their quarrels make your life a Hell,
      Your death a hope.

God send you find not such an end
  To ills however sharp and huge!
God send you convalesce! God send
  You vermifuge.

Shapes of Clay 4:165–68.

■

EGOTIST, *n*.

A person of low taste, more interested in himself than in me.

Megaceph, chosen to serve the State
In the halls of legislative debate,
One day with all his credentials came
To the capitol's door and announced his name.
The doorkeeper looked, with a comical twist
Of the face, at the eminent egotist,
And said: "Go away, for we settle here
All manner of questions, knotty and queer,
And we cannot have, when the speaker demands
To be told how every member stands,
A man who to all things under the sky
Assents by eternally voting 'I.' "

The Devil's Dictionary 7:81.

RIGHT, *n*.

Legitimate authority to be, to do or to have; as the right to be a king, the right to do one's neighbor, the right to have measles, and the like. The first of these rights was once universally believed to be derived directly from the will of God; and this is still sometimes affirmed *in partibus infidelium* outside the enlightened realms of Democracy; as the well known lines of Sir Abednego Bink, following:

> By what right, then, do royal rulers rule?
>> Whose is the sanction of their state and pow'r?
> He surely were as stubborn as a mule
>> Who, God unwilling, could maintain an hour
> His uninvited session on the throne, or air
> His pride securely in the Presidential chair.
>
> Whatever is is so by Right Divine;
>> Whate'er occurs, God wills it so. Good land!
> It were a wondrous thing if His design
>> A fool could baffle or a rogue withstand!
> If so, then God, I say (intending no offence)
> Is guilty of contributory negligence.

The Devil's Dictionary 7:295.

■

INFRALAPSARIAN, *n*.

One who ventures to believe that Adam need not have sinned unless he had a mind to—in opposition to the Supralapsarians, who hold that that luckless person's fall was decreed from the beginning. . . .

> Two theologues once, as they wended their way
> To chapel, engaged in colloquial fray—
> An earnest logomachy, bitter as gall,

Concerning poor Adam and what made him fall.
" 'Twas Predestination," cried one—"for the Lord
Decreed he should fall of his own accord."
"Not so—'twas Free will," the other maintained,
"Which led him to choose what the Lord had ordained."
So fierce and so fiery grew the debate
That nothing but bloodshed their dudgeon could sate;
So off flew their cassocks and caps to the ground
And, moved by the spirit, their hands went round.
Ere either had proved his theology right
By winning, or even beginning, the fight,
A gray old professor of Latin came by,
A staff in his hand and a scowl in his eye,
And learning the cause of their quarrel (for still
As they clumsily sparred they disputed with skill
Of foreordinational freedom of will)
Cried: "Sirrahs! this reasonless warfare compose:
Atwixt ye's no difference worthy of blows.
The sects ye belong to—I'm ready to swear
Ye wrongly interpret the names that they bear.
You—Infralapsarian son of a clown!—
Should only contend that Adam slipped down;
While *you*—you Supralapsarian pup!—
Should nothing aver but that Adam slipped up."

It's all the same whether up or down
You slip on a peel of banana brown.
Even Adam analyzed not his blunder,
But thought he had slipped on a peal of thunder!

G. J.

The Devil's Dictionary 7:163–65.

CONTROVERSY, *n.*

A battle in which spittle or ink replaces the injurious cannon-ball
and the inconsiderate bayonet.

In controversy with facile tongue—
That bloodless warfare of the old and young—
So seek your adversary to engage
That on himself he shall exhaust his rage,
And, like a snake that's fastened to the ground,
With his own fangs inflict the fatal wound.
You ask me how this miracle is done?
Adopt his own opinions, one by one,
And taunt him to refute them; in his wrath
He'll sweep them pitilessly from his path.
Advance then gently all you wish to prove,
Each proposition prefaced with, "As you've
So well remarked," or, "As you wisely say,
And I cannot dispute," or, "By the way,
This view of it which, better far expressed,
Runs through your argument." Then leave the rest
To him, secure that he'll perform his trust
And prove your views intelligent and just.

Conmore Apel Brune.

The Devil's Dictionary 7:55–56.

ABRACADABRA

By *Abracadabra* we signify
　　An infinite number of things.
'Tis the answer to What? and How? and Why?
And Whence? and Whither?—a word whereby
　　The Truth (with the comfort it brings)
Is open to all who grope in night,
Crying for Wisdom's holy light.

Whether the word is a verb or a noun
　　Is knowledge beyond my reach.
I only know that 'tis handed down
　　　　From sage to sage,
　　　　From age to age
　　An immortal part of speech!

Of an ancient man the tale is told
That he lived to be ten centuries old,
　　　　In a cave on a mountain side.
　　　　(True, he finally died.)
The fame of his wisdom filled the land,
For his head was bald, and you'll understand
　　　　His beard was long and white
　　　　And his eyes uncommonly bright.

Philosophers gathered from far and near
To sit at his feet and hear and hear,
　　　　Though he never was heard
　　　　To utter a word
But *"Abracadabra abracadab*
　　　Abracada, abracad,
Abrac abrac, abra, ab!"
　　　　'Twas all he had,

'Twas all they wanted to hear, and each
Made copious notes of the mystical speech,
Which they published next—
A trickle of text
In a meadow of commentary.
Mighty big books were these,
In number, as leaves of trees;
In learning, remarkable, very!

He's dead,
As I said,
And the books of the sages have perished,
But his wisdom is sacredly cherished.
In *Abracadabra* it solemnly rings,
Like an ancient bell that forever swings.
O, I love to hear
That word make clear
Humanity's General Sense of Things.

Jamrach Holobom.

The Devil's Dictionary 7:13–14.

SOMETHING IN THE PAPERS

"What's in the paper?" O, it's dev'lish dull:
There's nothing happening at all—a lull
After the war-storm. Mr. Someone's wife
Killed by her lover with, I think, a knife.
A fire on Blank Street and some babies—one,
Two, three or four, I don't remember, done
To quite a delicate and lovely brown.
A husband shot by woman of the town—
The same old story. Shipwreck somewhere south,
The crew all saved—or lost. Uncommon drouth
Makes hundreds homeless up the River Mud—
Though, come to think, I guess it was a flood.
'Tis feared some bank will burst—or else it won't;
They always burst I fancy—or they don't;
Who cares a cent?—the banker pays his coin
And takes his chances. Bullet in the groin—
But that's another item. Suicide—
Fool lost his money (serve him right) and died.
Heigh-ho! there's noth— Jerusalem! what's this?
Tom Jones has failed! My God, what an abyss
Of ruin!—owes me seven hundred, clear!
Was ever such a damned disastrous year?

Shapes of Clay 4:327.

INAUSPICIOUSLY, *adv.*

In an unpromising manner, the auspices being unfavorable. Among the Romans it was customary before undertaking any important action or enterprise to obtain from the augurs, or state prophets, some hint of its probable outcome; and one of their favorite and most trustworthy modes of divination consisted in observing the flight of birds—the omens thence derived being called *auspices*. . . .

A Roman slave appeared one day
Before the Augur. "Tell me, pray,
If—" here the Augur, smirking, made
A checking gesture and displayed
His open palm, which plainly itched,
For visibly its surface twitched.
A *denarius* (the Latin nickel)
Successfully allayed the tickle,
And then the slave proceeded: "Please
Inform me whether Fate decrees
Success or failure in what I
To-night (if it be dark) shall try.
Its nature? Never mind—I think
'Tis writ on this"—and with a wink
Which darkened half the earth, he drew
Another denarius to view,
Its shining face attentive scanned,
Then slipped it into the good man's hand,
Who with great gravity said: "Wait
While I retire to question Fate."
That holy person then withdrew
His sacred clay and, passing through
The temple's rearward gate, cried "Shoo!"
Waving his robe of office. Straight

Each sacred peacock and its mate
(Maintained for Juno's favor) fled
With clamor from the trees o'erhead,
Where they were perching for the night.
The temple's roof received their flight,
For thither they would always go,
When danger threatened them below.
Back to the slave the Augur went:
"My son, forecasting the event
By flight of birds, I must confess
The auspices deny success."
That slave retired, a sadder man,
Abandoning his secret plan—
Which was (as well the crafty seer
Had from the first divined) to clear
The wall and fraudulently seize
On Juno's poultry in the trees.

G. J.

The Devil 's Dictionary 7:155–56.

■

INSECTIVORA, *n.*

"See," cries the chorus of admiring preachers,
"How Providence provides for all His creatures!"
"His care," the gnat said, "even the insects follows:
For us He has provided wrens and swallows."

Sempen Railey.

The Devil's Dictionary 7:169.

THE NEW DECALOGUE

Have but one God: thy knees were sore
If bent in prayer to three or four.

Adore no images save those
The coinage of thy country shows.

Take not the Name in vain. Direct
Thy swearing unto some effect.

Thy hand from Sunday work be held—
Work not at all unless compelled.

Honor thy parents, and perchance
Their wills thy fortunes may advance.

Kill not—death liberates thy foe
From persecution's constant woe.

Kiss not thy neighbor's wife. Of course
There's no objection to divorce.

To steal were folly, for 'tis plain
In cheating there is greater gain.

Bear not false witness. Shake your head
And say that you have "heard it said."

Who stays to covet ne'er will catch
An opportunity to snatch.

Black Beetles in Amber 5:233.

THE BINNACLE

The Church possesses the unerring compass whose
needle points directly and persistently to the star
of the eternal law of God.—*Religious Weekly.*

The Church's compass, if you please,
Has two or three (or more) degrees
   Of variation;
And many a soul has gone to grief
On this or that or t'other reef
Through faith unreckoning or brief
   Miscalculation.
Misguidance is of perils chief
   To navigation.

The obsequious thing makes, too, you'll mark,
Obeisance through a little arc
   Of declination;
For Satan, fearing witches, drew
From Death's pale horse, one day, a shoe,
And nailed it to his door to undo
   Their machination.
Since then the needle dips to woo
   His habitation.

Shapes of Clay 4:328.

CHRISTIAN, *n.*

One who believes that the New Testament is a divinely in-
spired book admirably suited to the spiritual needs of his
neighbor. One who follows the teachings of Christ in so far as
they are not inconsistent with a life of sin.

I dreamed I stood upon a hill, and, lo!
The godly multitudes walked to and fro
Beneath, in Sabbath garments fitly clad,
With pious mien, appropriately sad,
While all the church bells made a solemn din—
A fire-alarm to those who lived in sin.
Then saw I gazing thoughtfully below,
With tranquil face, upon that holy show
A tall, spare figure in a robe of white,
Whose eyes diffused a melancholy light.

"God keep you, stranger," I exclaimed. "You are
No doubt (your habit shows it) from afar;
And yet I entertain the hope that you,
Like these good people, are a Christian too."
He raised his eyes and with a look so stern
It made me with a thousand blushes burn
Replied—his manner with disdain was spiced:
"What! I a Christian? No, indeed! I'm Christ."

G. J.

The Devil's Dictionary 7:49–50.

JUDEX JOCOSUS

We blench when maniacs to dance begin.
What makes a skull so dreadful is the grin.
When horrible and ludicrous unite,
Our sense of humor does but feed our fright.
As the shocked spirit with a double dread
Might see a monkey watching by the dead,
Or headsman part a neck, without a fault,
While turning o'er the block a somersault.
So, Judge Hilario, the untroubled awe
And reverence men cherish for the law
Turn all to terror when with wit profound
And tricksy humor *you* the law expound.
More frightful sounds the felon's doom by half
From lips still twisted to an idiot laugh.

Shapes of Clay 4:150.

LAW, *n.*

Once Law was sitting on the bench,
    And Mercy knelt a-weeping.
"Clear out!" he cried, "disordered wench!
    Nor come before me creeping.
Upon your knees if you appear,
'Tis plain you have no standing here."

Then Justice came. His Honor cried:
    "*Your* status?—devil seize you!"
"*Amica curiae,*" she replied—
    "Friend of the court, so please you."
"Begone!" he shouted—"there's the door—
I never saw your face before!"

                        G. J.

The Devil's Dictionary 7:186.

■

AN ERROR

"I never have been able to determine
Just how it is that the judicial ermine
Is safely guarded from predacious vermin."
"It is not so, my friend; though in a garret
'Tis kept in camphor, and you often air it,
The vermin will get into it and wear it."

The Scrap Heap 4:361.

UNEXPOUNDED

On Evidence, on Deeds, on Bills,
On Copyhold, on Loans, on Wills,
Lawyers great books indite.
The creaking of their busy quills
    I never heard on Right.

The Scrap Heap 4:366.

■

ORTHOGRAPHY, *n.*

The science of spelling by the eye instead of the ear. Advo-
cated with more heat than light by the outmates of every asy-
lum for the insane. They have had to concede a few things
since the time of Chaucer, but are none the less hot in defence
of those to be conceded hereafter.

A spelling reformer indicted
For fudge was before the court cicted.
    The judge said: "Enough—
    His candle we'll snough,
And his sepulchre shall not be whicted."

The Devil's Dictionary 7:240–41.

INCURABLE

From pride, guile, hate, greed, melancholy—
From any kind of vice, or folly,
Bias, propensity or passion
That is in prevalence and fashion,
Save one, the sufferer or lover
May, by the grace of God, recover.
Alone that spiritual tetter,
The zeal to make creation better,
Glows still immedicably warmer.
Who knows of a reformed reformer?

Shapes of Clay 4:228.

■

THE PUN

Hail, peerless Pun! thou last and best,
Most rare and excellent bequest
Of dying idiot to the wit
He died of, rat-like, in a pit!

Thyself disguised, in many a way,
Thou let'st thy sudden splendor play,
Adorning all where'er it turns,
As the revealing bull's-eye burns
For the dim thief, and plays its trick
Upon the lock he means to pick.

Yet sometimes, too, thou dost appear
As boldly as a brigadier
Tricked out with marks and signs all o'er

Of rank, brigade, division, corps,
To show by every means he can
An officer is not a man;
Or naked, with a lordly swagger,
Proud as a cur without a wagger,
Who says: "See simple worth prevail—
All dog, sir—not a bit of tail!"
'Tis then men give thee loudest welcome,
As if thou wert a soul from Hell come.

O obvious Pun! thou hast the grace
Of skeleton clock without a case—
With its whole boweling displayed,
And all its organs on parade.

Dear Pun, thou'rt common ground of bliss,
Where *Punch* and I can meet and kiss;
Than thee my wit can stoop no lower—
No higher his does ever soar.

Shapes of Clay 4:228–29.

■

MONTEFIORE

I saw—'twas in a dream the other night—
A man whose hair with age was thin and white:
    One hundred years had bettered by his birth,
And still his step was firm, his eye was bright.

Before him and about him pressed a crowd.
Each head in reverence was bared and bowed,

And Jews and Gentiles in a hundred tongues
Extolled his deeds and spoke his fame aloud.

I joined the throng and, pushing forward, cried,
"Montefiore!" with the rest, and vied
     In efforts to caress the hand that ne'er
To want and worth had charity denied.

So closely round him swarmed our shouting clan
He scarce could breathe, and taking from a pan
     A gleaming coin, he tossed it o'er our heads,
And in a moment was a lonely man!

Shapes of Clay 4:265; Stedman 444.

■

A TRENCHER-KNIGHT

Stranger, uncover; here you have in view
The monument of Chauncey M. Depew,
Eater and orator, the whole world round
For feats of tongue and tooth alike renowned.

Dining his way to eminence, he rowed
With knife and fork up water-ways that flowed
From lakes of favor—pulled with all his force
And found each river sweeter than the source.

Like rats, obscure beneath a kitchen floor,
Gnawing and rising till obscure no more,
He ate his way to eminence, and Fame
Inscribes in gravy his immortal name.

A trencher-knight, he, mounted on his belly,

So spurred his charger that its sides were jelly.
Grown desperate at last, it reared and threw him,
And Indigestion, overtaking, slew him.

Some Ante-Mortem Epitaphs 4:351–52.

■

COMPLIANCE

Said Rockefeller, senior, to his boy:
"Be good and you shall have eternal joy."
Said Rockefeller, junior, to his dad:
"I never do a single thing that's bad."
Said Rockefeller, senior—long gone gray
In service at the altar: "Ever pray."
And Rockefeller, junior, being bid,
Upon his knees and neighbors ever did.

Black Beetles in Amber 5:219.

■

A LITERARY METHOD

His "Hoosier poems" Riley says he writes
    Upon an empty stomach. Heavenly Powers,
Feed him throat-full; for what the wretch indites
    Upon his empty stomach empties ours!

The Scrap Heap 4:372.

DIES IRÆ

A recent republication of the late Gen. John A. Dix's disappointing translation of this famous medieval hymn, together with some researches into its history, which I happened to be making at the time, induces me to undertake a translation myself. It may seem presumption in me to attempt that which so many eminent scholars of so many generations have attempted before me; but failure of others encourages me to hope that success, being still unachieved, is still achievable. The fault of many translations, from Lord Macaulay's to that of Gen. Dix, has been, I venture to think, a too strict literalness, whereby the delicate irony and subtle humor of the immortal poem—though doubtless these admirable qualities were valued by the translators—have been sacrificed in the result. In none of the English versions that I have examined is more than a trace of the mocking spirit of insincerity pervading the whole prayer,—the cool effrontery of the suppliant in enumerating his demerits, his serenely illogical demands of salvation in spite, or rather because, of them, his meek submission to the punishment of others, and the many similarly pleasing characteristics of this amusing work being most imperfectly conveyed. By permitting myself a reasonable freedom of rendering—in many cases boldly supplying that "missing link" between the sublime and the ridiculous which the

Dies Iræ

Dies iræ! dies illa!
Solvet sæclum in favilla
Teste David cum Sibylla.

Quantus tremor est futurus,
Quando Judex est venturus,
Cuncta stricte discussurus.

author, writing for the acute monkish apprehension of the thirteenth century, did not deem it necessary to insert—I have hoped at least partly to liberate the lurking devil of humor from his letters, letting him caper, not, certainly, as he does in the Latin, but as he probably would have done had his creator written in English. In preserving the meter and trochaic rhymes of the original, I have acted from the same reverent regard for the music with which, in the liturgy of the Church, the verses have become inseparably wedded that inspired Gen. Dix; seeking rather to surmount the obstacles to success by honest effort, than to avoid them by adopting an easier versification which would have deprived my version of all utility in religious service.

I must bespeak the reader's charitable consideration in respect of the first stanza, the insuperable difficulties of which seem to have been purposely contrived in order to warn off trespassers at the very boundary of the alluring domain. I have got over the inhibition—somehow—but David and the Sibyl must try to forgive me if they find themselves represented merely by the names of those conspicuous personal qualities to which they probably owed their powers of prophecy, as Samson's strength lay in his hair.

The Day of Wrath

Day of Satan's painful duty!
Earth shall vanish, hot and sooty;
So says Virtue, so says Beauty.

Ah! what terror shall be shaping
When the Judge the truth's undraping—
Cats from every bag escaping!

Tuba mirum spargens sonum
Per sepulchra regionem,
Coget omnes ante thronum.

Mors stupebit, et Natura,
Quum resurget creatura
Judicanti responsura.

Liber scriptus proferetur,
In quo totum continetur,
Unde mundus judicetur.

Judex ergo quum sedebit,
Quicquid latet apparebit,
Nil inultum remanebit.

Quid sum miser tunc dicturus,
Quem patronem rogaturus,
Quum vix justus sit securus?

Rex tremendæ majestatis,
Qui salvandos salvas gratis;
Salva me, Fons pietatis.

Recordare, Jesu pie,
Quod sum causa tuæ viæ;
Ne me perdas illa die.

Quærens me sedisti lassus
Redemisti crucem passus,
Tantus labor non sit cassus,

Juste Judex ultionis,
Donum fac remissionis
Ante diem rationis.

Now the trumpet's invocation
Calls the dead to condemnation;
All receive an invitation.

Death and Nature now are quaking,
And the late lamented, waking,
In their breezy shrouds are shaking.

Lo! the Ledger's leaves are stirring,
And the Clerk, to them referring,
Makes it awkward for the erring.

When the Judge appears in session,
We shall all attend confession,
Loudly preaching non-suppression.

How shall I then make romances
Mitigating circumstances?
Even the just must take their chances.

King whose majesty amazes,
Save thou him who sings thy praises;
Fountain, quench my private blazes.

Pray remember, sacred Saviour,
Mine the playful hand that gave your
Death-blow. Pardon such behavior.

Seeking me, fatigue assailed thee,
Calvary's outlook naught availed thee;
Now 'twere cruel if I failed thee.

Righteous judge and learnèd brother,
Pray thy prejudices smother
Ere we meet to try each other.

Ingemisco tanquam reus,
Culpa rubet valtus meus;
Supplicanti parce, Deus.

Qui Mariam absolvisti,
Et latronem exaudisti,
Mihi quoque spem dedisti.

Preces meæ non sunt dignæ,
Sed tu bonus fac benigne
Ne perenni cremer igne.

Inter oves locum præsta.
Et ab hædis me sequestra,
Statuens in parte dextra.

Confutatis maledictis,
Flammis acribus addictis,
Voca me cum benedictis.

Oro supplex et acclinis,
Cor contritum quasi cinis;
Gere curam mei finis.

Lacrymosa dies illa
Qua resurget et favilla,
Judicandus homo reus,
Huic ergo parce, Deus!

Sighs of guilt my conscience gushes,
And my face vermilion flushes;
Spare me for my pretty blushes.

Thief and harlot, when repenting,
Thou forgavest—complimenting
Me with sign of like relenting.

If too bold is my petition
I'll receive with due submission
My dismissal—from perdition.

When thy sheep thou hast selected
From the goats, may I, respected,
Stand amongst them undetected.

When offenders are indicted,
And with trial-flames ignited,
Elsewhere I'll attend if cited.

Ashen-hearted, prone and prayerful,
When of death I see the air full,
Lest I perish too be careful.

On that day of lamentation,
When, to enjoy the conflagration,
Men come forth, O be not cruel:
Spare me, Lord—make them thy fuel.

Shapes of Clay 4:320–25; *San Francisco News Letter
and California Advertiser*, June 24, 1876.

MATTER FOR GRATITUDE

[Especially should we be thankful for having escaped the
ravages of the yellow scourge by which our neighbors have
been so sorely afflicted.—*Governor Stoneman's Thanksgiving
Proclamation.*]

Be pleased, O Lord, to take a people's thanks
That Thine avenging sword has spared our ranks—
That thou hast parted from our lips the cup
And forced our neighbors' lips to drink it up.
Father of Mercies, with a heart contrite
We thank Thee that Thou goest south to smite,
And sparest San Francisco's loins, to crack
Thy lash on Hermosillo's bleeding back—
That o'er our homes Thine awful angel spread
A friendly wing, and Guaymas weeps instead.

We praise Thee, God, that Yellow Fever here
His horrid banner has not dared to rear,
Consumption's jurisdiction to contest,
Her dagger deep in every second breast!
Catarrh and Asthma and Congestive Chill
Attest Thy bounty and perform Thy will.
These native messengers obey Thy call—
They summon singly, but they summon all.
Not, as in Mexico's impested clime,
Can Yellow Jack commit recurring crime.
We thank Thee that Thou killest all the time.

Thy tender mercies, Father, never end:
Upon all heads Thy blessings still descend,
Though their forms vary. Here the sown seeds yield
Abundant grain that whitens all the field—

There the smit corn stands barren on the plain,
Thrift reaps but straw and Famine gleans in vain.
Here the fat priest to the contented king
Points to the harvest and the people sing—
There mothers eat their offspring. Well, at least
Thou hast provided offspring for the feast.
An earthquake here rolls harmless through the land,
And Thou art good because the chimneys stand—
There templed cities sink into the sea,
And damp survivors, shrieking as they flee,
Skip to the hills and hold a celebration
In honor of Thy wise discrimination.

O God, forgive them all, from Stoneman down,
Thy smile who construe and expound Thy frown,
And fall with saintly grace upon their knees
To render thanks when Thou dost only sneeze.

Black Beetles in Amber 5:31–33.

JUDEX JUDICATUS

Judge Armstrong, when the poor have sought your aid,
To be released from vows that they have made
In haste, and leisurely repented, you,
As stern as Rhadamanthus (Minos too,
And Æacus) have drawn your fierce brows down
And petrified them with a moral frown!
With iron-faced rigor you have made them run
The gauntlet of publicity—each Hun
And Vandal of the public press allowed
To throw their households open to the crowd
And bawl their secret bickerings aloud.
When Wealth before you suppliant appears,
Bang! go the doors and open fly your ears!
The blinds are drawn, the lights diminished burn,
Lest eyes too curious should look and learn
That gold refines not, sweetens not, a life
Of conjugal brutality and strife—
That vice is vulgar, though it gilded shine
Upon the curve of a judicial spine.
The veiled complainant's whispered evidence,
The plain collusion and the no defense,
The sealed exhibits and the secret plea,
The unreported and unseen decree,
The midnight signature and—*chink! chink! chink!*
Nay, pardon, upright Judge, I did but think
I heard that sound abhorred of honest men;
No doubt it was the scratching of your pen.

O California! long-enduring land,
Where Judges fawn upon the Golden Hand,
Proud of such service to that rascal thing

As slaves would blush to render to a king—
Judges, of judgment destitute and heart,
Of conscience conscious only by the smart
From the recoil (with caution-bump enlarged)
Of duty accidentally discharged—
Invoking still a "song o' sixpence" from
The Scottish fiddle of each lusty palm,—
Thy Judges, California, skilled to play
This silent music, through the livelong day,
Perform obsequious before the rich,
And still the more they scratch the more they itch!

Black Beetles in Amber 5:222–23.

A GROWLER

Judge Shafter, you're an aged man, I know,
    And learned too, I doubt not, in the law;
And a head white with many a winter's snow
    (I wish, however, that your heart would thaw)
    Claims reverence and honor; but the jaw
That's always busy with a word malign,
    Nagging and scolding every one in sight
As harshly as a jaybird in a pine,
    And with as little sense of wrong and right
As animates that irritable creature,
Is not a very venerable feature.

You damn all witnesses, all jurors too,
    And swear at the attorneys, I suppose
(But that's a far more righteous thing to do)
    And what it's all about, the good Lord knows,
    Not you; but all the hotter, fiercer glows
Your wrath for that—as dogs the louder howl
    With only moonshine to incite their rage,
And bears with more ferocious menace growl,
    Even when their food is flung into the cage.
Reform, your Honor, and forbear to curse us,
Lest all men, hearing you, cry: *"Ecce ursus!"*

Black Beetles in Amber 5:280–81.

TO A BULLY

They say, George Perry, you're a lawyer. Well,
    At least that's your profession, but in fact,
Law's like religion (though, the truth to tell,
    The likeness is not otherwise exact)
In this, that in them both, my learned brother,
Profession's one thing, practice quite another.

But you do practice, for the other day
    I saw you mentioned in a case in court,
Cross-questioning a witness. I must say
    You did it as a cat that loves to sport
With an unworthy mouse all too unwilling
To accept the justice of repeated killing.

This witness, so the tale is told to me,
    Fatigued of your attempt upon his life—
I mean his reputation—made him free
    With yours, affirming that you beat your wife.
If that is true (they say that it upset you)
She must be monstrous cowardly to let you!

You hold it right to torture men who come
    (Heaven knows unwillingly) to aid the law,
So that by terror of your tongue made dumb
    They can't tell rightly what they heard or saw.
"Impeaching credibility," you call it
When, seeing an honest looking head, you maul it.

Well, witnesses are fallible—involved
    Sometimes in scandals; and 'tis true that they
Are factors in the problem to be solved,
    The judge and jury led by what they say.

But lawyers—they are factors too, their problem
Being foolish clients and how best to rob them.

They've more to say than witnesses, and more
    Important 'tis that they be truthful, too.
Were't not, then, right the witness take the floor
    And mercilessly cross-examine *you*?
Were truth your jewel (bless us! what a setting!)
I've certain questions that would set you sweating!

Nay, don't be fidgeting; to ask them here
    Were perilous, for I no license hold
To be a blackguard; and no judge is near
    To jail you for replies too sharp and bold.
Besides, it were no easy task to shame you,
And till I'm paid a fee I'll not defame you.

You see I lack advantages that you
    Possess, and therefore cannot be so brave.
Who has, and uses, them's respected; who
    Has not, yet bullies, is a scurril knave—
Though, faith, the difference is narrow, very,
By which a knave's distinguished from a Perry.

You served, if rightly I remember, once
    A term in the State Legislature, where
You figured merely as a harmless dunce,
    Save when, ambitious, in the larger air
Of rhetoric you held the floor a season
To give yourself for sin sufficient reason.

Thus a great bird whose nature is in doubt
    With difficulty rises from the earth,

His wide wings spreading with an effort out,
    And shows by his unconscionable girth
E'er yet the agitated air insult your
Resentful nose, he's but a glutted vulture.

Touching these matters I would fain inquire
    If I but had you on the witness-grill,
Over the slow but efficacious fire
    Of cross-examination; and I'd kill
The worm with quite insensible gradation,
And quench the fire with great deliberation.

What, you're no worse than other lawyers? Well,
    I never said you were, my little man.
Do you suppose I run this private Hell
    For one small soul? 'Tis your entire clan
I'm trying to barbecue, despite their pleadings.
Get out, you brat! you hamper the proceedings!

Black Beetles in Amber 5:215–18.

■

TO AN INSOLENT ATTORNEY

So, Hall McAllister, you'll not be warned—
My protest slighted, admonition scorned!
To save your scoundrel client from a cell
As loth to swallow him as he to swell
Its sum of meals insurgent (it decries
All wars intestinal with meats that rise)
You turn your scurril tongue against the press
And damn the agency you ought to bless.
Had not the press with all its hundred eyes

Discerned the wolf beneath the sheep's disguise
And raised the cry upon him, he to-day
Would lack your company, and you would lack his pay.

Talk not of "hire" and consciences for sale—
You whose profession 'tis to threaten, rail,
Calumniate and libel at the will
Of any villain who can pay the bill,—
You whose most honest dollars all were got
By saying for a fee "the thing that's not!"
To you 'tis one, to challenge or defend;
Clients are means, their money is an end.
In my profession sometimes, as in yours
Always, a payment large enough secures
A mercenary service to defend
The guilty, or the innocent to rend.
But mark the difference, nor think it slight:
We do not hold it proper, just and right;
Of selfish lies a little still we shame
And give our villainies another name.
Hypocrisy's an ugly vice, no doubt,
But blushing sinners can't get on without.
Happy the lawyer!—at his favored hands
Nor truth nor decency the world demands.
Secure in his immunity from shame,
His cheek ne'er kindles with the tell-tale flame.
His brains for sale, morality for hire,
In every land and century a licensed liar!
No doubt, McAllister, you can explain
How honorable 'tis to lie for gain,
Provided only that the jury's made
To understand that lying is your trade.

A hundred thousand volumes, broad and flat,
(The Bible not included) proving that,
Have been put forth, though still the doubt remains
If God has read them with befitting pains.
No Morrow could get justice, you'll declare,
If none who knew him foul affirmed him fair.
Ingenious man! how easy 'tis to raise
An argument to justify the course that pays!

I grant you, if you like, that men may need
The services performed for crime by greed,—
Grant that the perfect welfare of the State
Requires the aid of those who in debate
As mercenaries lost in early youth
The fine distinction between lie and truth,—
Who cheat in argument and set a snare
To take the feet of Justice unaware,—
Who serve with livelier zeal when rogues assist
With perjury, embracery (the list
Is long to quote) than when an honest soul,
Scorning to plot, conspire, intrigue, cajole,
Reminds them (their astonishment how great!)
He'd rather suffer wrong than perpetrate.
I grant, in short, 'tis better all around
That ambidextrous consciences abound
In courts of law to do the dirty work
That self-respecting scavengers would shirk.
What then? Who serves however clean a plan
By doing dirty work, he is a dirty man!

Black Beetles in Amber 5:240–42.

GENESIS

God said: "Let there be Man," and from the clay
Adam came forth and, thoughtful, walked away.
The matrix whence his body was obtained,
An empty man-shaped cavity, remained
All unregarded from that early time
Till in a modern storm it filled with slime.
Now Satan, envying his Master's power
To make the meat himself could but devour,
Strolled to the place and, standing by the pool,
Exerted all his will to make a fool.
A miracle!—from out that ancient hole
Rose Morehouse, lacking nothing but a soul.
"To give him that I've not the power divine,"
Said Satan, sadly, "but I'll lend him mine."
He breathed it into him, a vapor black,
And to this day has never got it back.

Black Beetles in Amber 5:49.

■

FINIS ÆTERNITATIS

Strolling at sunset in my native land,
With fruits and flowers thick on either hand,
    I crossed a Shadow flung athwart my way,
Emerging on a waste of rock and sand.

"The apples all are gone from here," I said,
"The roses perished and their spirits fled.
    I will go back." A voice cried out: "The man
Is risen who eternally was dead!"

I turned and saw an angel standing there,
Newly descended from the heights of air.
    Sweet-eyed compassion filled his face, his hands
A naked sword and golden trumpet bare.

"Nay, 'twas not death, the shadow that I crossed,"
I said. "Its chill was but a touch of frost.
    It made me gasp, but quickly I came through,
With breath recovered ere it scarce was lost."

'Twas the same land! Remembered mountains thrust
Grayed heads asky, and every dragging gust,
    In ashen valleys where my sons had reaped,
Stirred in familiar river-beds the dust.

Some heights, where once the traveler was shown
The youngest and the proudest city known,
    Lifted smooth ridges in the steely light—
Bleak, desolate acclivities of stone.

Where I had worshiped at my father's tomb,
Within a massive temple's awful gloom,
    A jackal slunk along the naked rock,
Affrighted by some prescience of doom.

Man's vestiges were nowhere to be found,
Save one brass mausoleum on a mound
    (I knew it well) spared by the artist Time
To emphasize the desolation round.

Into the stagnant sea the sullen sun
Sank behind bars of crimson, one by one.
    "Eternity's at hand!" I cried aloud.
"Eternity," the angel said, "is done.

"For man is ages dead in every zone;
The angels all are dead but I alone;
    The devils, too, are cold enough at last,
And God lies dead before the great white throne!

" 'Tis foreordained that I bestride the shore
When all are gone (as Gabriel did before,
    When I had throttled the last man alive)
And swear Eternity shall be no more."

"O Azrael—O Prince of Death, declare
Why conquered I the grave?" I cried. "What rare,
    Conspicuous virtues won this boon for me?"
"You've been revived," he said, "to hear me swear."

"Then let me creep again beneath the grass,
And knock you at yon pompous tomb of brass.
    If ears are what you want, Charles Crocker's there—
Betwixt the greatest ears, the greatest ass."

He rapped, and while the hollow echoes rang,
Out at the door a curst hyena sprang
    And fled! Said Azrael: "His soul's escaped,"
And closed the brazen portal with a bang.

Black Beetles in Amber 5:65–67.

A WORD TO THE UNWISE

[Charles Main, of the firm of Main & Winchester, has ordered
a grand mausoleum for his plot in Mountain View Cemetery.
—*City Newspaper*.]

Charles Main, of Main & Winchester, attend
With friendly ear the chit-chat of a friend
    Who knows you not, yet knows that you and he
Travel two roads that have a common end.

We journey forward through the time allowed,
I humbly bending, you erect and proud.
    Our heads alike will stable soon the worm—
The one that's lifted, and the one that's bowed.

You in your mausoleum shall repose,
I where it pleases Him who sleep bestows;
    What matter whether one so little worth
Shall stain the marble or shall feed the rose?

Charles Main, I had a friend who died one day.
A metal casket held his honored clay.
    Of cyclopean architecture stood
The splendid vault where he was laid away.

A dozen years, and lo! the roots of grass
Had burst asunder all the joints; the brass,
    The gilded ornaments, the craven stones
Lay tumbled all together in a mass.

A dozen years! That taxes your belief.
Make it a thousand if the time's too brief.
    'Twill be the same to you; when you are dead
You cannot even count our days of grief.

Suppose a pompous monument you raise
Till on its peak the solar splendor blaze
    While yet about its base the night is black;
But will it give your glory length of days?

Say, when beneath, your rubbish has been thrown,
Some rogue to reputation all unknown—
    Men's backs being turned—should lift his thieving
        hand,
Efface your name and substitute his own,

Whose then would be the monument? To whom
Would be the fame? Forgotten in your gloom—
    Your very name forgotten!—ah, my friend,
The name is all that's rescued by the tomb.

For memory of worth and work we go
To other records than a stone can show.
    These lacking, naught remains; with these
The stone is needless for the world will know.

Then build your mausoleum if you must,
And creep into it with a perfect trust;
    But in the twinkling of an eye the plow
Shall pass without obstruction through your dust.

Another movement of the pendulum,
And, lo! the desert-haunting wolf shall come,
    And, seated on the spot, shall howl by night
O'er rotting cities, desolate and dumb.

Black Beetles in Amber 5:173–75.

POLITICAL ECONOMY

"I beg you to note," said a Man to a Goose,
As he plucked from her bosom the plumage all loose,
"That pillows and cushions of feathers, and beds
As warm as maids' hearts and as soft as their heads,
Increase of life's comforts the general sum—
Which raises the standard of living." "Come, come,"
The Goose said impatiently, "tell me or cease,
How that is of any advantage to geese."
"What, what!" said the man—"you are very obtuse!
Consumption no profit to those who produce?
No good to accrue to Supply from a grand
Progressive expansion, all around, of Demand?
Luxurious habits no benefit bring
To those who purvey the luxurious thing?
Consider, I pray you, my friend, how the growth
Of luxury promises—" "Promises," quoth
The sufferer, "what?—to what course is it pledged
To pay me for being so often defledged?"
"Accustomed"—this notion the plucker expressed
As he ripped out a handful of down from her breast—
"To one kind of luxury, people soon yearn
For others and ever for others in turn.
The man who to-night on your feathers will rest,
His mutton or bacon or beef to digest,
His hunger to-morrow will wish to assuage
With goose and a dressing of onions and sage."

Shapes of Clay 4:215–16.

THE BRIDE

"You know, my friends, with what a brave carouse
I made a second marriage in my house—
　　Divorced old barren Reason from my bed
And took the Daughter of the Vine to spouse."

So sang the Lord of Poets. In a gleam
Of light that made her like an angel seem,
　　The Daughter of the Vine said: "I myself
Am Reason, and the Other was a Dream."

Shapes of Clay 4:329; Stedman 443.

GRAPE, *n*.

Hail noble fruit!—by Homer sung,
    Anacreon and Khayyám;
Thy praise is ever on the tongue
    Of better men than I am.

The lyre my hand has never swept,
    The song I cannot offer:
My humbler service pray accept—
    I'll help to kill the scoffer.

The water-drinkers and the cranks
    Who load their skins with liquor—
I'll gladly bare their belly-tanks
    And tap them with my sticker.

Fill up, fill up, for wisdom cools
    When e'er we let the wine rest.
Here's death to Prohibition's fools,
    And every kind of vine-pest!

Jamrach Holobom.

The Devil's Dictionary 7:121–22.

THE MORMON QUESTION

By J–QU–N M–LL–R

I said I will shake myself out of my clothes,
I will roll up my sleeves, I will spit on my hands
(The hands that I kissed to the sun in the lands
To the north, to the east, to the south, and the west
Of every sea that is under the sun),
I will go to the land that the Gentile loathes
As he gathers his one small wife to his breast
And curses and loathes till his life is done.
I will go to the place of the Mormon: the place
Where the jackass rabbit is first in the race
And the woodchuck chatters in meaningless glee—
Chatters and twists all his marvelous face—
Twists it and chatters and looks like me.
And I rose in the strongest strength of my strength,
With my breast of brass and my hair's full length,
And I shook myself out of my clothes in the land
Of the Mormons, and stood there and kissed my hand.

Black Beetles in Amber 5:304.

■

THE PERVERTED VILLAGE

After Goldsmith

Sweet Auburn! liveliest village of the plain,
Where Health and Slander welcome every train,
Whence smiling innocence, its tribute paid,
Retires in terror, wounded and dismayed—

Dear lovely bowers of gossip and disease,
Whose climate cures us that thy dames may tease,
How often have I knelt upon thy green
And prayed for death, to mitigate their spleen!
How often have I paused on every charm
With mingled admiration and alarm—
The brook that runs by many a scandal-mill,
The Church whose pastor groans upon the grill,
The cowthorn bush with seats beneath the shade,
Where hearts are struck and reputations flayed;
How often wished thine idle wives, some day,
Might more at whist, less at the devil, play.

Unblest retirement! ere my life's decline
(Killed by detraction) may I witness thine.
How happy she who, shunning shades like these,
Finds in a wolf-den greater peace and ease;
Who quits the place whence truth did earlier fly,
And rather than come back prefers to die;
For her no jealous maids renounce their sleep,
Contriving malices to make her weep;
No iron-faced dames her character debate
And spurn imploring mercy from the gate;
But down she lies to a more peaceful end,
For beasts don't vilify, they only rend—
Sinks piecemeal to their maws, a willing prey,
While resignation lubricates the way,
And all her prospects brighten at the last:
To wolves, not women, an approved repast.

Black Beetles in Amber 5:148–49; *San Francisco Wasp,* July 5,
1884.

A POSSIBILITY

If the wicked gods were willing
    (Pray it never may be true!)
That a universal chilling
    Should ensue
Of the sentiment of loving,—
    If they made a great undoing
Of the plan of turtle-doving,
        Then farewell all poet-lore,
            Evermore.
If there were no more of billing
    There would be no more of cooing
And we all should be but owls—
        Lonely fowls
Blinking wonderfully wise,
    With our great round eyes—
Sitting singly in the gloaming and no longer two and two
As unwilling to be wedded as unpracticed how to woo;
    With regard to being mated,
    Asking still with aggravated
Ungrammatical acerbity: "To who? To who?"

Shapes of Clay 4:109–10.

THE KING OF BORES

Abundant bores afflict this world, and some
    Are bores of magnitude that come and—no,
    They're always coming, but they never go—
Like funeral pageants, as they drone and hum
Their lurid nonsense like a muffled drum,
    Or bagpipe's dread, unnecessary flow.
    But one superb tormentor I can show—
Prince Fiddlefaddle, Duc de Feefawfum.
He the johndonkey is who, when I pen
    Amorous verses in an idle mood
        To nobody, or of her, reads them through
And, smirking, says he knows the lady; then
    Calls me sly dog. I wish he understood
        This tender sonnet's application too.

Shapes of Clay 4:313–14; *San Francisco Wasp,* November 4, 1881.

■

TO NANINE

Dear, if I never saw your face again;
    If all the music of your voice were mute
    As that of a forlorn and broken lute;
If only in my dreams I might attain
The benediction of your touch, how vain
    Were Faith to justify the old pursuit
    Of happiness, or Reason to confute
The pessimist philosophy of pain.
Yet Love not altogether is unwise,

For still the wind would murmur in the corn,
    And still the sun would splendor all the mere;
    And I—I could not, dearest, choose but hear
Your voice upon the breeze and see your eyes
    Shine in the glory of the summer morn.

Shapes of Clay 4:230.

■

NANINE

We heard a song-bird trilling—
    'Twas but a day ago.
Such rapture he was rilling
    As only we could know.

This morning he is flinging
    His music from the tree,
But something in the singing
    Is not the same to me.

His inspiration fails him,
    Or he has lost his skill.
Nanine, Nanine, what ails him
    That he should sing so ill?

Nanine is not replying—
    She hears no earthly song.
The sun and bird are lying
    And the night is, O, so long!

Shapes of Clay 4:139.

ONE MORNING

Because that I am weak, my love, and ill
    I cannot follow the impatient feet
    Of my desire, but sit and watch the beat
Of the unpitying pendulum fulfill
The hour appointed for the air to thrill
    And brighten at your coming. O my sweet,
    The tale of moments is at last complete—
The tryst is broken on the gusty hill!
O lady, faithful-footed, loyal-eyed,
    The long leagues silence me; yet doubt me not:
Think rather that the clock and sun have lied
    And all too early you have sought the spot.
For lo! despair has darkened all the light
And till I see your face it still is night.

Shapes of Clay 4:313.

TO MAUDE

Not as two errant spheres together grin
    With monstrous ruin in the vast of space,
    Destruction born of that malign embrace,
Their hapless peoples all to death consigned—
Not so when our intangible worlds of mind,
    Even mine and yours, each with its spirit race,
    Of beings shadowy in form and face,
Shall drift together on some blessed wind.
No, in that marriage of gloom and light
    All miracles of beauty shall be wrought,
      Attesting a diviner faith than man's;
For all my sad-eyed daughters of the night
    Shall smile on your sweet seraphim of thought,
      Nor any jealous god forbid the banns.

Shapes of Clay 4:200.

ON STONE

As in a dream, strange epitaphs I see,
　　Inscribed on yet unquarried stone,
　　Where wither flowers yet unstrown—
The Campo Santo of the time to be.

On Stone 5:373.

■

Here Salomon's body reposes;
Bring roses, ye rebels, bring roses.
Set all of your drumsticks a-moving,
Discretion and Valor approving;
Discretion—he always retreated—
And Valor—the dead he defeated.
Bring roses, ye loyal, bring roses:
As patriot here he re-poses.

On Stone 5:378.

■

Cynic perforce from studying mankind
In the false volume of his single mind,
He damned his fellows for his own unworth,
And, bad himself, thought nothing good on earth.
Yet, still so judging, and so erring still,
Observing well, but understanding ill,
His learning all was got by dint of sight,
And what he knew by day he lost by night.
When hired to flatter he would never cease

Till those who'd paid for praises paid for peace.
Not wholly miser and but half a knave,
He yearned to squander but he lived to save,
And did not, for he could not, cheat the grave.
Hic jacet Pixley, scribe and muleteer:
Step lightly, stranger, anywhere but here.

On Stone 5:374–75.

■

Here lies the last of Deacon Fitch,
Whose business was to melt the pitch.
Convenient to this sacred spot
Like Sammy, who applied it hot.
'Tis hard—so much alike they smell—
One's grave from t'other's grave to tell,
But when his tomb the Deacon's burst
(Of two he'll always be the first)
He'll see by studying the stones
That he's obtained his proper bones,
Then, seeking Sammy's vault, unlock it,
And put that person in his pocket.

On Stone 5:380.

LORING PICKERING

(After Pope)

Here rests a writer, great but not immense,
Born destitute of feeling and of sense.
No power he but o'er his brain desired—
How not to suffer it to be inspired.
Ideas unto him were all unknown,
Proud of the words which only were his own.
So unreflecting, so confused his mind,
Torpid in error, indolently blind,
A fever Heaven to quicken him applied,
But rather than revive, the sluggard died.

On Stone 5:373.

■

For those this mausoleum is erected
Who Stanford to the Upper House elected.
Their luck is less or their promotion slower,
For, dead, they were elected to the Lower.

On Stone 5:376.

■

Here Stanford lies, who thought it odd
That he should go to meet his God.
He looked, until his eyes grew dim,
For God to hasten to meet him.

On Stone 5:381.

George Perry here is stiff and stark,
>   With stone at foot and stone at head.
His heart was dark, his mind was dark—
>   "Ignorant ass!" the people said.

Not ignorant but skilled, alas,
>   In all the secrets of his trade:
He knew more ways to be an ass
>   Than any ass that ever brayed.

On Stone 5:379.

■

McAllister, of talents rich are rare,
>   Lies at this spot at finish of his race.
Alike to him if it is here or there:
>   The one spot that he cared for was the ace.

On Stone 5:375.

Uncollected Poems

BASILICA

With aimless feet, along the verge
Of ocean, where the rocks emerge,
I strolled, and watched the baffled surge.

In sheltered channels at my feet,
The sleepy ripples crisping neat,
Slid in and out with sluicy beat.

The groaning sea, wind-smitten white—
The day, shot through with throbbing light,
Lay palpitating on my sight.

From bloody death of stricken day,
And ocean's leprous agony,
My weary eyes I drew away,

To where the rocks the margin mar
Of waters where the shadows are—
And saw the smiling of a star.

Imbedded deep in mossy green,
A glinting gem with lustrous sheen
Burnt wondrous with a flame serene.

My soul grew drunken with its ray—
Like liquid April filling May,
Its wing-light suffused the day.

And day became—with colors cold
New-drowned in beauties manifold—
An opal chalice brimming gold.

A silent music clove the air—
A spirit bent in worship there—
My wish had wrought itself a prayer.

"O, if thy beauty, radiant stone,
Be not rejected love alone,
By wooing stars upon thee thrown;

"But rather a desire intense
Appealing thus to human sense
With more than human eloquence;

"If so thou strivest to impart
The aspirations at thy heart—
Pulsing a wish with every spark;

"Give me to claim thy sacred ray;
I'll bear thee from thy shades away,
And set thee in the perfect day.

"I'll niche thee in a shrine made fair
With wondrous woods and metals rare,
And dim with amber-tinted air;

"And sculpted work of quaint device,
Gem-tinct with gleams of prismic ice,
And lamps antique of fabled price.

"And droning troops of monkish bees,
With censers filled at spicy trees,
Shall minister on bended knees."

Grey darkness fell upon the land;
With hasty clutch my eager hand
To snatch the gem from barren strand

Essayed. When, Lo! with stiffened hair—
And vision smit with baleful glare—
And hope sharp-freezing to despair—

With heart compressed as in a vice,
And forehead bound with sudden ice—
I grasped a hidden Cockatrice:

O, with Heart of Stone, with eyes of light,
And ivory throat of pallid white,
And snaky folds concealed from sight;

With jeweled teeth, alas! and breath
Whose touch to passion ministreth—
Sweet-spiced with aromatic death!

No pen of poison, gall-immersed,
Of deadly sins can name thy worst;
Or fitly curse thy race accursed.

San Francisco, September 16th, 1867.

The Californian, September 21,
1867; Sidney-Fryer 33–35.

A MYSTERY

A thing to be thought with abated breath,
    And named with Tears:
There ever shall be as there ever have been,
Beyond our ken,
        The weight of the Past with its burden of sin,
        A shadow thrown from the Future within,
On the souls of men.
And the weight unfelt and the shadow unseen,
With the cry of the Present unheard between,
        Is all of life.
And 'tis only through toil and the nameless pain
Of wishes forever unwished again,
        By an aimless strife,—
As who should do battle with weapon of steel
To the fleshless Dark which he cannot feel,
        As it hedges him round—
        That peace is found.
Thinkest thou that "to smile" is the same as "to live,"
That a life shall receive what it need not give,
        That toil is toil;
That a fruitful future unmoistened by tears
Brings harvest of ears,
        And wine and oil?
O, Dreamer of Dreams, there forever shall be
A blossomless growth in the spirit of thee
        Still draping in gloom
Each fairy façade of each castle so fair,
By thy fancy upreared in the roseate air,
        As ivy a tomb,

'Tis rooted in life and its fruit is of death,
    And the poisoned breath,
In its baleful shadow, still shudders and moans
    In voiceless tones.
Wouldst thou know, O mortal, the secret of Pain?
'Tis the payment in blood for each wish we obtain.

San Francisco, November 18, 1867.

The Californian, November 23, 1867; Sidney-Fryer 36–37.

ROSALIE

Lithesome, blithesome daughter mine,
Lift to me those lips of thine;
Greet me with those eyes of blue,
Eyes which seem to look me through:
Flashing now with life and light;
    Now in hush of sleep reposing,
Veiled by lashes dark as night—
    Shadows over violets closing.
Come thou, o'er me softly bow,
    Shower on me fond caresses;
O'er my cheek, and on my brow,
    Fling thy wealth of sunbright tresses.
Every throbbing pulse of mine
Beats in time and tune to thine;
All my heart's tide sets to thee,
Loving little Rosalie.

As the dewdrop doth the flower,
As the sunshine doth the hour,
So the music of thy voice
Makes my soul rejoice.
All the livelong day around
    Babbles on thy childlike chatter;
Mingled with the pleasant sound
    Comes thy little foot's light patter.
Like the linnet's on the thorn
    Joyously thy carol floweth—
Sing, my bird, for thy young morn
    No dark night of winter knoweth.
Blue-eyed romp, in ceaseless whirl,
Half the angel, half the girl,

All the child art thou to me,
Laughing little Rosalie.

Loved one mine, the sunny day
Passeth rapidly away;
All too soon the bright time goes—
All too fast life's current flows.
Now its fairy waters glide
    Where the sunbeams o'er it quiver;
Soon the salt waves meet its tide,
    Soon the beck will be the river—
Thine is now the primrose spring,
    Thine the bluebell in the meadows:
Mine the fading hours that fling
    Autumn leaves and lengthening shadows;
Yet my day lights up awhile
'Neath the sunshine of thy smile—
Thou dost bring new life to me,
Lithesome, blithesome Rosalie.

San Francisco News Letter and California Advertiser, December 25, 1869, p. 2.

TO THEE, MY DARLING

The heliotrope's fragrant breath—
The subtle sweet of jasmine on the evening air—
The flowery mead, all radiant
With sympathetic pleasure
From the glowing kiss with which
The God of Day salutes its lovely face—
The whispering, snowy surf, wherewith
Old Ocean in his kindliest mood
Murmurs soft secrets to the willing sands—
The mingled joy and anguish thrilling us
In the weird plaints of Schubert—
Great Rossini's heaven-born strains—
All graceful, lovely things,
Lifting my soul to beatific state,—
Mnemosyne with flowery fetters
Binds to thee, my darling.

*San Francisco News Letter and California
Advertiser* 20 (February 26, 1870): 8.

■

SERENADE

Listen, maiden, to my strain,
    Listen, pray thee, do!
Darkness shrouds the gloomy plain,
And our moon is on the wane,
Yet this fog cools not my brain,
    'Tis on fire anew.

List! and from thy couch arise,
    Rise, dear, pray thee do!
Not to gaze on murky skies,
That were now nor well nor wise,
But because your lover tries
    To catch sight of you!

Draw that dismal curtain back—
    Draw it back, duck, do!
'Tis like these clouds, whose flimsy rack
Hides yon bright moon's silvery track,
I'd rather *see* the window black,
    And know it bright to you.

Let me see those love-lit eyes—
    Let me, sweet; now, do-o-o!
Lit by them these misty skies
Ne'er would wish the moon to rise,
And the stars, like scared fire-flies,
    Would hide deep in the blue.

Come, dear, dup that tiresome door—
    Dup the door, duck, do-oo-o!
Let me love afar no more,
Singing in the fog's a bore,
Sooth to say my throat is sore,
    Hoarse I'm getting too.

Let me to thy chamber creep,
    Let me creep up, do-oo-oo!
I'll not again disturb thy sleep,
Nor more before thy window weep,
Listen, love, and do not keep
    Me longer in the dew.

Listen, maiden, to my song,
>Listen, now come, do-oo-oo-oo!
Do not deem my rhyming wrong,
I'm not of the ribald throng,
Let me in, I merely long
>To read my rhymes to you.

San Francisco, March 16, 1870.

San Francisco News Letter and California Advertiser 20 (March 19, 1870), 16.

■

SCIENCE

The winds of heaven trample down the pines
>Or creep in lazy tides along the lea;
Lead the wild waters from the smitten rock,
>Or crawl with childish babble to the sea;
But why the tempests out of heaven blow,
Or what the purpose of the seaward flow,
No man hath known, and none shall ever know.

Why seek to know? To follow nature up
>Against the current of her course, why care?
Vain is the toil; he's wisest still who knows
>All science is but formulated prayer—
Prayer for the warm winds and the quickening rain,
Prayer for sharp sickle and for laboring swain,
To gather from the planted past the grain.

Golden Era, December, 1893. Reprinted in Ella Sterling Mighels, ed., *Literary California* (San Francisco: Harr Wagner, 1918), 243.

HOW BLIND IS HE

How blind is he who, powerless to discern
The glories that around his pathway burn,
Walks unaware the avenues of Dream
Nor sees the domes of Paradise agleam!
O Golden Age, to him more nobly planned
Thy light lies ever upon sea and land.
From sordid scenes he lifts his eyes at will
And sees a Grecian god on every hill.

T. H. Reardon, ed., *Petrarch and Other Essays* (San Francisco: William Doxey, 1893); photographic copy of Bierce MS published in Vincent Starrett, *Ambrose Bierce: A Bibliography* (Philadelphia: Centaur Book Shop, 1929), 44.

■

MY DAY OF LIFE

I know not how it is—it seems
    Fantastic and surprising
That after all these dreams and dreams,
Here in the sun's first level beams,
    The sun is still just rising!

When first he showed his sovereign face,
    And bade the night-folk scuttle
Back to their holes, I took my place
Here on the hill, and God His grace
    Sent slumber soft and subtle.

Among the poppies red and white,
    I've lain and drowsed, for all it
Appears a sluggardly delight.

I must have had a wakeful night,
    Though, faith, I don't recall it.

And, O I've dreamed so many things!
    One hardly can unravel
The tangled web of visionings
That slumber-of-the-morning brings:
    Play, study, work and travel;

The love of women (mostly those
    Were fairest that were newest);
Hard knocks from friends and other foes:
Compacts with men (my memory shows
    The deadest are the truest);

War—what a hero I became
    By merely dreaming battle!
Athwart the field of letters, Fame
Blared through the brass my weary name
    With an ominous death-rattle.

Such an eternity of thought
    Within a minute's fraction!
Such phantoms out of nothing wrought,
And fading suddenly to naught
    As I awake to action!

They scamper each into its hole,
    These dreams of my begetting.
They've had their moment; take, my soul,
Thy day of life. . . . Gods! this is droll—
    That thieving sun is "setting"!

Oakland, September 3 [1910].

San Francisco Town Talk, September 10, 1910, p. 10.

About Poetry

The Matter of Manner

I have sometimes fancied that a musical instrument retains among its capabilities and potentialities something of the character, some hint of the soul, some waiting echo from the life of each who has played upon it: that the violin which Paganini had touched was not altogether the same afterward as before, nor had quite so fine a fibre after some coarser spirit had stirred its strings. Our language is a less delicate instrument: it is not susceptible to a debasing contagion; it receives no permanent and essential impress but from the hand of skill. You may fill it with false notes, and these will speak discordant when invoked by a clumsy hand; but when the master plays they are all unheard—silent in the quickened harmonies of masters who have played before.

My design is to show in the lucidest way that I can the supreme importance of words, their domination of thought, their mastery of character. Had the Scriptures been translated, as literally as now, into the colloquial speech of the unlearned, and had the originals been thereafter inaccessible, only direct interposition of the Divine Power could have saved the whole edifice of Christianity from tumbling to ruin.

Max Muller distilled the results of a lifetime of study into two lines:

No language without Reason.
No Reason without Language.

The person with a copious and obedient vocabulary and the will and power to apply it with precision thinks great thoughts. The mere glib talker—who may have a meagre vocabulary and no sense of discrimination in the use of words—is another kind of creature. A nation whose language is strong and rich and flexible and sweet—such as English was just before the devil invented dictionaries—has a noble literature and, compared with contemporary nations barren in speech, a superior morality. A word is a crystallized thought; good words are precious possessions, which nevertheless, like gold, may be mischievously used. The introduction of a bad word, its preservation, the customary misuse of a good one—these are sins affecting the public welfare. The fight against faulty diction is a fight against insurgent barbarism—a fight for high thinking and right living—for art, science, power—in a word, civilization. A motor without mechanism; an impulse without a medium of transmission; a vitalizing thought with no means to impart it; a fertile mind with a barren vocabulary—than these nothing could be more impotent. Happily they are impossible. They are not even conceivable.

Conduct is of character, character is of thought, and thought is unspoken speech. We think in words; we can not think without them. Shallowness or obscurity of speech means shallowness or obscurity of thought. Barring a physical infirmity, an erring tongue denotes an erring brain. When I stumble in my speech I stumble in my thought. Those who have naturally the richest and most obedient vocabulary are also the wisest thinkers; there is little worth knowing but what they have thought. The most brutish savage is he who is most meagrely equipped with words; fill him with words to the top of his gift and you would make him as wise as he is able to become.

The man who can neither write well nor talk well would have us believe that, like the taciturn parrot of the anecdote, he is "a devil to think." It is not so. Though such a man had read the Alexandrian library he would remain ignorant; though he had sat at the feet of Plato he would be still unwise. The gift of expression is the measure of mental capacity; its degree of cultivation is the exponent of intellectual power. One may choose not to utter one's mind—that is another matter; but if he choose he can. He can utter it all. His mind, not his heart; his thought, not his emotion. And if he do not sometimes choose to utter he will eventually cease to think. A mind without utterance is like a lake without an outlet: though fed with mountain springs and unfailing rivers, its waters do not long keep sweet.

Human speech is an imperfect instrument—imperfect by reason of its redundancy, imperfect by reason of its poverty. We have too many words for our meaning, too many meanings for our words. The effect is so confusing and embarrassing that the ability to express our thoughts with force and accuracy is extremely rare. It is not a gift, but a gift and an accomplishment. It comes not altogether by nature, but is achieved by hard, technical study.

In illustration of the poverty of speech take the English word "literature." It means the art of writing and it means the things written—preferably in the former sense by him who has made it a study, almost universally in the latter by those who know nothing about it. Indeed, the most of these are unaware that it has another meaning, because unaware of the existence of the thing which in that sense it means. Tell them that literature, like painting, sculpture, music, and architecture, is an art—the most difficult of arts—and you must expect an emphatic dissent. The denial not infrequently comes from persons of wide reading, even wide writing, for the popular writer commonly utters his ideas as, if he pursued the vocation for which he is better fitted, he would dump another kind of rubbish from another kind of cart—pull out the tailboard and let it go. The immortals have a different method.

Among the minor trials of one who has a knowledge of the art of literature is the book of one who has not. It is a light affliction, for he need not read it. The worthy bungler's conversation about the books of others is a sharper disaster, for it can not always be evaded and must be courteously endured; and, goodness gracious! how comprehensively he does not know! How eagerly he points out the bottomless abyss of his ignorance and leaps into it! The *censor literarum* is perhaps the most widely distributed species known to zoology.

The ignorance of the reading public and the writing public concerning literary art is the eighth wonder of the world. Even its rudiments are to these two great classes a thing that is not. From neither the talk of the one nor the writing of the other would a student from Mars ever learn, for illustration, that a romance is not a novel; that poetry is a thing apart from the metrical form in which it is most acceptable; that an epigram is not a truth tersely stated—is, in fact, not altogether true; that fable is neither story nor anecdote; that the speech of an illiterate doing the best he knows how is another thing than dialect; that prose has its prosody no less exacting than verse. The ready-made critic and the ready-made writer are two of a kind and each is good enough for the other. To both, writing is writing, and that is all there is of it. If we had two words for the two things now covered by the one word "literature" perhaps the benighted could be taught to distinguish between, not only the art and the product, but, eventually, the different kinds of the product itself. As it is, they are in much the same state of darkness as that of the Southern young woman before she went North and learned, to her astonishment, that the term "damned Yankee" was two words—she had never heard either without the other.

In literature, as in all art, manner is everything and matter nothing; I mean that matter, however important, has nothing to do with the *art* of literature; that is a thing apart. In literature it makes very little difference what you say, but a great deal how you say it. It is precisely this thing called style which determines and fixes the place of any written discourse; the thoughts may be the most interesting, the statements the most important, that it is possible to conceive; yet if they be not cast in the literary mold, the world can not be persuaded to accept the work as literature. What could be more important and striking than the matter of Darwin's books, or Spencer's? Does anyone think of Darwin and Spencer as men of letters? Their manner, too, is admirable for its purpose—to convince. Conviction, though, is not a literary purpose. What can depose Sterne from literature? Yet who says less than Sterne, or says it better?

It is so in painting. One man makes a great painting of a sheepcote; another, a bad one of Niagara. The difference is not in the subject—in that the Niagara man has all the advantage; it is in the style. Art—literary, graphic, or what you will—is not a matter of matter, but a matter of manner. It is not the What but the How. The master enchants when writing of a pebble on the beach; the bungler wearies us with a storm at sea. Let the dullard look to his theme and thought; the artist sets down what comes. He pickles it sweet with a salt savor of verbal felicity, and it charms like Apollo's lute.

The Opinionator 10:57–64.

Edwin Markham's Poems

In Edwin Markham's book, *The Man with the Hoe and Other Poems,* many of the "other poems" are excellent, some are great. If asked to name the most poetic—not, if you please, the "loftiest" or most "purposeful"—I think I should choose "The Wharf of Dreams." I venture to quote it:

> Strange wares are handled on the wharves of sleep;
>> Shadows of shadows pass, and many a light
>> Flashes a signal fire across the night;
> Barges depart whose voiceless steersmen keep
> Their way without a star upon the deep;
>> And from lost ships, homing with ghostly crews,
>> Come cries of incommunicable news,
> While cargoes pile the piers a moon-white heap—
> Budgets of dream-dust, merchandise of song,
> Wreckage of hope and packs of ancient wrong,
> Nepenthes gathered from a secret strand,
>> Fardels of heartache, burdens of old sins,
>> Luggage sent down from dim ancestral inns,
> And bales of fantasy from No-Man's Land.

Really, one does not every year meet with a finer blending of imagination and fancy than this; and I know not where to put a finger on two better lines in recent work than these:

> And from lost ships, homing with ghostly crews,
> Come cries of incommunicable news.

The reader to whom these strange lines do not give an actual physical thrill may rightly boast himself impregnable to poetic emotion and indocible to the meaning of it.

Mr. Markham has said of Poetry—and said greatly:

She comes like the hush and beauty of the night,
    And sees too deep for laughter,
Her touch is a vibration and a light
    From worlds before and after.

But she comes not always so. Sometimes she comes with a burst of music, sometimes with a roll of thunder, a clash of weapons, a roar of winds, or a beating of billow against the rock. Sometimes with a noise of revelry, and again with the wailing of a dirge. Like Nature, she "speaks a various language." Mr. Markham, no longer content, as once he seemed to be, with interpreting her fluting and warbling and "sweet jargoning," learned to heed her profounder notes, which stir the stones of the temple like the bass of a great organ.

In his "Ode to a Grecian Urn" Keats has supplied the greatest—almost the only truly great instance of a genuine poetic inspiration derived from art instead of nature. In his poems on pictures Mr. Markham shows an increasingly desperate determination to achieve success, coupled with a lessening ability to merit it. It is all very melancholy, the perversion of this man's high powers to the service of a foolish dream by artificial and impossible means. Each effort is more ineffectual than the one that went before. Unless he can be persuaded to desist—to cease interpreting art and again interpret nature, and turn also from the murmurs of "Labor" to the music of the spheres—the "surge and thunder" of the universe—the end of his good literary repute is in sight. He knows—does he know?—the bitter truth which he might have learned otherwise than by experience: that the plaudits of "industrial discontent," even when strengthened by scholars' commendations of a few great lines in the poem that evoked it, are not fame. He should know, and if he live long will know, that when one begins to be a "labor leader" one ceases to be a poet.

In saying to Mr. Markham, "Thou ailest here and here," Mrs. Atherton has shown herself better at diagnosis than he is himself in telling us what is the matter with the rich. "Why," she asks him, "waste a beautiful gift in groveling for popularity with the mob? . . . Striving to please the common mind has a fatal commonizing effect on the writing faculty." It is even so—nothing truer could be said, and Mr. Markham is the best proof of its truth. His early work, when he was known to only a small circle of admirers, was so good that I predicted for him the foremost place among contemporaneous American poets. He sang because he "could not choose but sing," and his singing grew greater and greater. Every year he took wider outlooks from "the peaks of song" —had already got well above the fools' paradise of flowers and song-birds and bees and women and had invaded the "thrilling region" of the cliff, the eagle, and the cloud, whence one looks down upon man and out upon the world. Then he had the mischance to publish "The Man with the Hoe," a poem with some noble lines, but an ignoble poem. In the first place, it is, in structure, stiff, inelastic, monotonous. One line is very like another. The cæsural pauses fall almost uniformly in the same places; the full stops always at the finals. Comparison of the versification with Milton's blank will reveal the difference of method in all its significance. It is a difference analogous to that between painting

on ivory and painting on canvas—between the dead, flat
tints of the one and the lively, changing ones due to inequal-
ities of surface in the other. If it seems a little exacting to
compare Mr. Markham's blank with that of the only poet
who has ever mastered that medium in English, I can only
say that the noble simplicity and elevation of Mr. Markham's
work are such as hardly to justify his admeasurement by any
standard lower than the highest that we have.

My chief objection relates to the sentiment of the piece,
the thought that the work carries; for although thought is
no part of the poetry conveying it, and, indeed, is almost al-
together absent from some of the most precious pieces (lyri-
cal, of course) in our language, no elevated composition has
the right to be called great if the message that it delivers is
neither true nor just. All poets, even the little ones, are
feelers, for poetry is emotional; but all the great poets are
thinkers as well. Their sympathies are as broad as the race,
but they do not echo the peasant's philosophies of the work-
shop and the field. In Mr. Markham's poem the thought is
that of the labor union—even to the workworn threat of ris-
ing against the wicked well-to-do and taking it out of their
hides.

> Who made him dead to rapture and despair,
> A thing that grieves not and that never hopes,
> Stolid and stunned, a brother to the ox?
> Who loosened and let down this brutal jaw?
> Whose was the hand that slanted back this brow?
> Whose breath blew out the light within this brain?

One is somehow reminded by these lines of Coleridge's
questions in the Chamouni hymn, and one is tempted to an-
swer them the same way: God. "The Man with the Hoe" is

not a product of the "masters, lords and rulers in all lands":
they are not, and no class of men is, accountable for him, his
limitations and his woes, which are not of those "that kings
or laws can cause or cure." The "masters, lords and rulers"
are as helpless "in the fell clutch of circumstance" as he—
which Mr. Markham would be speedily made to understand
if appointed Dictator. The notion that the sorrows of the
humble are due to the selfishness of the great is "natural,"
and can be made poetical, but it is silly. As a literary concep-
tion it has not the vitality of a sick fish. It will not carry a
poem of whatever excellence through two generations.
That a man of Mr. Markham's splendid endowments should
be chained to the body of this literary death is no less than a
public calamity.

For his better work in poetry Mr. Markham merits all the
praise that he has received for "The Man with the Hoe," and
more. It is not likely that he is now under any illusion in the
matter. He probably knows the real nature of his sudden
flare of "popularity"; knows that to-morrow it will be "one
with Nineveh and Tyre"; knows that its only service to him is
to arrest attention of competent critics and scholars who
would otherwise have overlooked him for a time. The "plau-
dits of the multitude" can not long be held by the poet, and
are not worth holding. The multitude knows nothing of po-
etry and does not read it. The multitude will applaud you to-
day, calumniate you to-morrow, and thwack you athwart the
mazzard the day after. He who builds upon the sea-sand of
its favor holds possession by a precarious tenure; the wind
veers and the wave

Lolls out his large tongue—
    Licks the whole labor flat.

If the great have left the humble so wise that the philoso-
phies of the factory and the plow-tail are true; if the senti-
ments and the taste of the mob are so just and elevated that
its judgment of poetry is infallible and its approval a pre-
cious possession; if "the masses" have more than "a thin ve-
neering of civilization," and are not in peace as fickle as the
weather and in anger as cruel as the sea; if these victims of an
absolutely universal oppression "in *all* lands" are deep, dis-
criminating, artistic, liberal, magnanimous—in brief, wise
and good—it is difficult to see what they have to complain
about. Mr. Markham, at least, is forbidden to weep for them,
for he is a lover of Marcus Aurelius, of Seneca, of Epictetus.
These taught, and taught truly—one from the throne of an
empire, one writing at a gold table, and one in the intervals
of service as a slave—the supreme value of wisdom and
goodness, the vanity of power and wealth, the triviality of
privation, discomfort, and pain. Mr. Markham is a disciple
of Jesus Christ, who from the waysides and the fields taught
that poverty is not only a duty, but indispensable to salva-
tion. So my *argumentum ad hominem* runs thus: The objects of
our poet's fierce invective and awful threats have suffered
his *protégés* to remain rather better off than they are them-
selves—have appropriated and monopolized only what is
not worth having. In view of this mitigating circumstance I
feel justified in demanding in their behalf a lighter sentence.
Let the portentous effigy of the French Revolution be for-
bidden to make faces at them.

I know of few literary phenomena more grotesque than
some of those growing out of "The Man with the Hoe"—
that sudden popularity being itself a thing which "goes
neare to be fonny." Mr. Markham, whom for many years
those of us who modestly think ourselves *illuminati* consid-

ered a great poet whose greatness full surely was a-ripening, wrote many things far and away superior to "The Man," but these brought him recognition from the judicious only, with which we would all have sworn that he was content. All at once he published a poem which, despite some of its splendid lines, is neither true in sentiment nor admirable in form—which is, in fact, addressed to peasant understandings and soured hearts. Instantly follow a blaze and thunder of notoriety, seen and heard over the entire continent; and even the coasts of Europe are "telling of the sound." Straightway before the astonished vision of his friends the author stands transfigured! The charming poet has become a demagogue, a "labor leader" spreading that gospel of hate known as "industrial brotherhood," a "walking delegate" diligently inciting a strike against God and clamoring for repeal of the laws of nature. Saddest of all, we find him conscientiously promoting his own vogue. He personally appears at meetings of cranks and incapables convened to shriek against the creed of law and order; speaks at meetings of sycophants eager to shine by his light; introduces lecturers to meetings of ninnies and femininnies convened to glorify themselves. When he is not waving the red flag of discontent and beating the big drum of revolution I presume he is resting—perched, St.–Simeon–Stylitiswise, atop a lofty capital I, erected in the market place, diligently and rapturously contemplating his new identity. All of which is very sad to those of us who find it difficult to unlove him.

The trouble with Mr. Markham is that he has formed the habit of thinking of mankind as divided on the property line—as comprising only two classes, the rich and the poor. When a man has acquired that habit he is lost to sense and righteousness. Assassins sometimes reform, and with increasing education thieves renounce the error of theft to embrace the evangel of embezzlement; but a demagogue never gets again into shape unless he becomes wealthy. I hope Mr. Markham's fame will so promote his pecuniary interest that it will convert him from the conviction that his birth was significantly coincident in point of time with the Second Advent. Only one thing is more disagreeable than a man with a mission, namely a woman with a mission, and the superior objectionableness of the latter is largely due to her trick of inspiring the former.

Mr. Markham seems now to look upon himself as the savior of society; to believe with entire sincerity that in his light and leading mankind can be guided out of the wilderness of Self into the promised land of Altruria; that he can alter the immemorial conditions of human existence; that a new Heaven and a new Earth can be created by the power of his song. Most melancholy of all, the song has lost its power and its charm. Since he became the Laureate of Demagogy he has written little that is poetry: in the smug prosperity that he reviles in others, his great gift "shrinks to its second cause and is no more." That in the great white light of inevitable disillusion he will recover and repossess it, giving us again the flowers and fruits of a noble imagination in which the dream of an impossible and discreditable hegemony has no part, I should be sorry to disbelieve.

1899.

The Reviewer 10:137–48.

England's Laureate

Doubtless there are competent critics of poetry in this country, but it is Mr. Alfred Austin's luck not to have drawn their attention. Mr. Austin is not a great poet, but he is a poet. The head and front of his offending seems to be that he is a lesser poet than his predecessor—his immediate predecessor—for his austerest critic will hardly affirm his inferiority to the illustrious Nahum Tate. Nor is Mr. Austin the equal by much of Mr. Swinburne, who as Poet Laureate was impossible—or at least highly improbable. If he had been offered the honor Mr. Swinburne would very likely have knocked off the Prime Minister's hat and jumped upon it. He is of a singularly facetious turn of mind, is Mr. Swinburne, and has to be approached with an orange in each hand.

Below Swinburne the differences in mental stature among British poets are inconsiderable; none is much taller than another, though Henley only could have written the great lines beginning,

> Out of the dark that covers me,
>> Black as the Pit from pole to pole,
> I thank whatever gods may be
>> For my unconquerable soul—

and he is not likely to do anything like that again; on that proposition

You your existence might put to the hazard and turn of
    a wager.

I wonder how many of the merry gentlemen who find a
pleasure in making mouths at Mr. Austin for what he does
and doesn't do have ever read, or reading, have understood,
his sonnet on

LOVE'S BLINDNESS

Now do I know that Love is blind, for I
    Can see no beauty on this beauteous earth,
    No life, no light, no hopefulness, no mirth,
Pleasure nor purpose, when thou art not nigh.
Thy absence exiles sunshine from the sky,
    Seres Spring's maturity, checks Summer's birth,
Leaves linnet's pipe as sad as plover's cry,
    And makes me in abundance find but dearth.
But when thy feet flutter the dark, and thou
    With orient eyes dawnest on my distress,
Suddenly sings a bird on every bough,
    The heavens expand, the earth grows less and less,
The ground is buoyant as the ether now,
    And all looks lovely in thy loveliness.

The influence of Shakespeare is altogether too apparent
in this, and it has as many faults as merits; but it is admirable
work, nevertheless. To a poet only come such conceptions as
"orient eyes" and feet that "flutter the dark."

Here is another sonnet in which the thought, quite as nat-
ural, is less obvious. In some of his best work Mr. Austin runs
rather to love (a great fault, madam) and this is called

LOVE'S WISDOM

Now on the summit of Love's topmost peak
    Kiss we and part; no further can we go;
    And better death than we from high to low
Should dwindle, and decline from strong to weak.
We have found all, there is no more to seek;
    All we have proved, no more is there to know;
And Time can only tutor us to eke
    Out rapture's warmth with custom's afterglow.
We cannot keep at such a height as this;
    For even straining souls like ours inhale
But once in life so rarefied a bliss.
    What if we lingered till love's breath should fail!
Heaven of my earth! one more celestial kiss,
    Then down by separate pathways to the vale.

Will the merry Pikes of the Lower Mississippi littoral and the gamboling whalebackers of the Duluth hinterland be pleased to say what is laughable in all this?

It is not to be denied that Mr. Austin has written a good deal of "mighty poor stuff," but I humbly submit that a writer is not to be judged by his poorest work, but by his best,—as an athlete is rated, not by the least weight that he has lifted, but by the greatest—not by his nearest cast of the discus, but by his farthest. Surely a poet, as well as a race-horse, is entitled to the benefit of his "record performance."

1903.

The Opinionator 10:113–16.

Who Are Great?

The question having been asked whether Abraham Lincoln was the greatest man this country ever produced, a contemporary writer signifies his own view of the matter thus:

"Abraham Lincoln was a great man, but I am inclined to believe that history will reckon George Washington a greater."

But that is an appeal to an incompetent arbiter. History has always elevated to primacy in greatness that kind of men—men of action, statesmen and soldiers. In my judgment neither of the men mentioned is entitled to the distinction. I should say that the greatest American that we know about, if not George Sterling, was Edgar Allan Poe. I should say that the greatest man is the man capable of doing the most exalted, the most lasting and most beneficial intellectual work—and the highest, ripest, richest fruit of the human intellect is indubitably great poetry. The great poet is the king of men; compared with him, any other man is a peasant; compared with his, any other man's work is a joke. What is it likely that remote ages will think of the comparative greatness of Shakespeare and the most eminent of all Britain's warriors or statesmen? Nothing, for knowledge of the latter's work will have perished. Who was the greatest of Grecians before Homer? Because you are unable to mention offhand the names of illustrious conquerors or empire-builders of the period do you suppose there were none?

Their work has perished, that is all—as will perish the work of Washington and Lincoln. But the *Iliad* is with us.

Their work has perished and our knowledge of it. Why? Because no greater man made a record of it. If Homer had celebrated their deeds instead of those of his dubious Agamemnon and impossible Achilles, we should know about them—all that he chose to tell. For a comparison between their greatness and his the data would be supplied by himself. Men of action owe their fame to men of thought. The glory of the ruler, the conqueror, or the statesman belongs to the historian or the poet who made it. He can make it big or little, at his pleasure; he upon whom it is bestowed is as powerless in the matter as is any bystander. If there were no writers how would you know that there was a Washington or a Lincoln? How would you know that there is a Joseph Choate, who was American Ambassador to Great Britain, or a Nelson Miles, sometime Commander of our army? Suppose the writers of this country had in 1896 agreed never again to mention the name of William J. Bryan; where would have been his greatness?

Great writers make great men or unmake them—or can if they like. They kindle a glory where they please, or quench it where it has begun to shine. History's final judgment of Washington and Lincoln will depend upon the will of the immortal author who chooses to write of them. Their deeds, although a thousand times more distinguished, their popularity, though a thousand times greater, can not save from oblivion even so much as their names. And nothing that they built will abide. Of the "topless towers" of empire that the one assisted to erect, and the other to buttress, not a vestige will remain. But what can efface "The Testimony of the Suns"? Who can unwrite "To Helen"?

If there had been no Washington, American independence would nevertheless have been won and the American republic established. But suppose that he alone had taken up arms. He was neither indispensable nor sufficient. Without Lincoln the great rebellion would have been subdued and negro slavery abolished. What kind of greatness is that—to do what another could have done, what was bound to be done anyhow? I call it pretty cheap work. Great statesmen and great soldiers are as common as flies; the world is lousy with them. We recognize their abundance in the saying that the hour brings the man. We do not say that of a literary emergency. There the demand is always calling for the supply, and usually calling in vain. Once or twice in a century, it may be, the great man of thought comes, unforeseen and unrecognized, and makes the age and the glory thereof all his own by saying what none but he could say—delivering a message which none but he could hear. All round him swarm the little great men of action, laying sturdily about them with mace and sword, changing boundaries which are afterward changed back again, serving fascinating principles from which posterity turns away, building states that vanish like castles of cloud, founding thrones and dynasties with which Time plays at pitch-and-toss. But through it all, and after it all, the mighty thought of the man of words flows on and on with the resistless sweep of "the great river where De Soto lies"—an unchanging and unchangeable current of eternal good.

> They say the Lion and the Lizard keep
> The courts where Jamshyd gloried and drank deep;
>   And Bahram, that great Hunter—the wild ass
> Stamps o'er his Head, but can not break his sleep.

But the courts that Omar reared still stand, perfect as when he "hewed the shaft and laid the architrave." Not the lion and the lizard—we ourselves keep them and glory in them and drink deep in them, as did he. O'er his head, too, that good man and considerable poet, Mr. Edgar Fawcett, stamped in vain; but a touch on a book, and lo! old Omar is broad awake and with him wakens Israfel, "whose heart-strings are a lute."

Art and literature are the only things of permanent interest in this world. Kings and conquerors rise and fall; armies move across the stage of history and disappear in the wings; mighty empires are evolved and dissolved; religions, political systems, civilizations flourish, die, and, except in so far as gifted authors may choose to perpetuate their memory, are forgotten and all is as before. But the thought of a great writer passes from civilization to civilization and is not lost, although his known work, his very name, may perish. You can not unthink a thought of Homer, but the deeds of Agamemnon are long undone, and the only value that he has, the only interest, is that he serves as material for poets. Of Cæsar's work only that of the pen survives. If a statue by Phidias, or a manuscript by Catullus, were discovered today the nations of Europe would be bidding against one another for its possession to-morrow—as one day the nations of Africa may bid for a newly discovered manuscript of some one now long dead and forgotten. Literature and art are about all that the world really cares for in the end; those who make them are not without justification in regarding themselves as masters in the House of Life and all others as their servitors. In the babble and clamor, the pranks and antics of its countless incapables, the tremendous dignity of the profession of letters is overlooked; but when, casting a retrospective eye into "the dark backward and abysm of time" to where beyond these voices is the peace of desolation, we note the majesty of the few immortals and compare them with the pigmy figures of their contemporary kings, warriors, and men of action generally—when across the silent battle fields and hushed *fora* where the dull destinies of nations were determined, nobody cares how, we hear,

> like ocean on a western beach,
> The surge and thunder of the Odyssey—

then we appraise literature at its true value; and how little worth while seems all else with which Man is pleased to occupy his fussy soul and futile hands!

1901.

The Controversialist 10:249–55.

Poetry and Verse

Love of poetry is universal, but this is not saying much; for men in general love it not as poetry, but as verse—the form in which it commonly finds utterance, and in which its utterance is most acceptable. Not that verse is essential to poetry; on the contrary, some of the finest poetry extant (some of the passages of the Book of Job, in the English version, for familiar examples) is neither metric nor rhythmic. I am not quite sure, indeed, but the best test of poetry yet discovered might not be its persistence or disappearance when clad in the garb of prose. In this opinion I differ, though with considerable reluctance, with General Lucius Foote, who asserts that "every feature which makes poetry to differ from prose is the result of expression." This dictum he has fortified by but a single example: he puts a stanza of Tennyson's "Charge of the Light Brigade" into very good prose. Now, for one who has at times come so perilously near to writing genuine poetry as has General Foote, this is a little too bad. Surely no man of so competent literary judgment ever before affected to believe that Tennyson's resonant patriotic lines were poetry, in any sense. They are, however, a little less distant from it in General Foote's prose version— "There were some cannons on the right, and some on the left, and some in front, and they fired with a great noise"— than they are in the original. And I have the hardihood to add that as a rule the "old favorites" of the lyceum—the ringing and rhetorical curled darlings of the public—the

"Address to the American Flag," "The Bells," the "Curfew Must Not Ring To-night," and all the ghastly lot of them, are very rubbishy stuff, indeed. There are exceptions, unfortunately, but to a cultivated taste—the taste of a mind that not only knows what it likes, but knows and can definitely state why it likes it—nine in ten of them are offensive. I say it is unfortunate there are exceptions. It is unfortunate as impairing the beauty and symmetry of the rule, and unfortunate for the authors of the exceptional poems, who must endure through life the consciousness that their popularity is a cruel injustice.

Far be it from me to underrate the value of the delicate and difficult art of managing words. It is to poetry what color is to painting. The thought is the outline drawing, which, if it be great, no dauber who stops short of actually painting it out can make wholly mean, but to which the true artist with his pigments can add a higher glory and a new significance. No one who has studied style as a science and endeavored to practice it as an art; no one who knows how to select with subtle skill the word for the place; who balances one part of his sentence against another; who has an alert ear for the harmony of stops, cadences and inflections, orderly succession of accented syllables and recurrence of related sounds—no one, in short, who knows how to write prose can hold in light esteem an art so nearly allied to his own as that of poetic expression, including as it does the intricate one of versification, which itself embraces such a multitude of dainty wisdoms. But expression is not all; while, on the one hand, it can no more make a poetic idea prosaic than it can make falsehood of truth, so, on the other, it is unable to elevate and beautify a sentiment essentially vulgar or base. The experienced miner will no more surely detect the presence of gold in the rough ore than a trained judgment the noble sentiment in the crude or ludicrous verbiage in which ignorance or humor may have cast it; and the terrier will with no keener nose penetrate the disguise of the rat that has rolled in a bed of camomile than the practiced intelligence detect the pauper thought masquerading in fine words. The mind that does not derive a quiet gratification from the bald statement that the course of the divine river Alph was through caves of unknown extent, whence it fell into a dark ocean, will hardly experience a thrill of delight when told by Coleridge that

Alph, the sacred river, ran
Through caverns measureless to man,
   Down to a sunless sea.

Nor would one who is capable of physically feeling the lines,

Full many a glorious morning have I seen
   Flatter the mountain tops with sovereign eye,

have disdained to be told by some lesser Shakspeare that he had observed mornings so fine that the mountains blushed with pleasure to be noticed by them. Poetry is too multiform and many-sided for anyone to dogmatize upon single aspects and phases of it as if they were the whole; it has as many shapes as Proteus, and as many voices as a violin. It sometimes thunders and sometimes it prattles; it shouts and exults, but on occasion it can whisper. Crude and harsh at one time, the voice of the muse is at another smooth, soft, exquisite, luxurious; and again scholarly and polite. There is ornate poetry, like the façade of a Gothic cathedral, and there is poetry like a Doric temple. Poems there are which blaze like a parterre of all brilliant flowers, and others as chaste and pallid as the white lily. It is all good (though I hasten to explain with some alarm that I do not think all verse is good) but the best minds are best agreed in awarding the palm to poetry that is most severely simple in diction—in which are fewest "inversions"—from which words of new coinage and compounding are rigorously excluded, and the old are used in their familiar sense; poetry, that is to say, that differs least in expression from the best prose. A truly poetic line—a line that I never tire of repeating to myself—is this from Byron:

> And the big rain comes dancing to the earth!

It is from the description of a storm in the Alps, in "Childe Harold." I will quote the whole stanza in order that the reader may be reminded how much of the excellence of this line depends upon its context:

> And this is in the night—most glorious night!
>> Thou wert not sent for slumber! let me be
> A sharer in thy fierce and far delight—
>> A portion of the tempest and of thee!
> How the lit lake shines, a phosphoric sea,
>> And the big rain comes dancing to the earth!
> And now again 'tis black—and now the glee
>> Of the loud hills shakes with its mountain-mirth,
> As if they did rejoice o'er a young earthquake's birth.

It would not be difficult, were it worth while, to point out in this stanza almost as many faults as it has lines; after the "lit lake" the "phosphoric sea"—a simile that repeats the image and debauches it—is singularly execrable, and the "young earthquake's birth" is almost as bad; but all the imperfections of the stanza count for nothing, for they are redeemed by its merits, and particularly by that one splendid line. Yet how could the thought it holds be more baldly stated? I only stipulate that the rain shall be "big," and "dancing" seem to be the manner of its approach. With these not very hard, and perfectly fair, conditions let ingenuity do its malevolent worst to vulgarize that thought. These few instances prove, I hope, that poetry, whatever it is, is something more than "words, words, words"—that there is such a thing as poetry of the thought.

But let us take a different kind of example. If poetry is all in the manner, as General Foote avers, expression must be able to create poetry out of anything; at least, no line has been drawn between the prosaic ideas upon which expression can work its miracle and those upon which it can not. I am, therefore, justified by a familiar law of logic in assuming that it is meant that expression, by the mere magic of method, can make *any* idea poetical. Now, I beg most respectfully to submit the following problems to be "worked out" by believers in that dictum: Make poetry of the thought that—

(1) Glue is made from the hoofs of cattle, and (2) silk purses by macerating the ears of sows in currant jelly.

If anyone will build a superstructure of poetry upon either of those "ideas" as a foundation I will be first and loudest in calling attention to the glory of the edifice.

I have said that men in general do not love poetry as poetry, but as verse. They are pleased with verse, but if the verse contain poetry they like it none the better for that. To the vast majority of the readers of even the higher class newspapers, verse and poetry are terms strictly synonymous. The pleasure they get from metre and rhyme is merely physical or sensual. It is much the same kind of pleasure as that derived from the clatter of a drum and the rhythmic clash of cymbals, and altogether inferior to the delight that the other instruments of a band produce. Emerson, I believe, accounts for our delight in metrical composition by supposing metre to have some close relation to the rhythmical recurrences within our physical organization—respiration, the pulse-beat, etc. No doubt he is right, and if so we need not take the trouble to deride the easy-going intellect that is satisfied with sound for sentiment whenever the sound is in harmony with the physical nature that perceives it, for in such sounds is a natural charm. The old lady who found so much Christian comfort in pronouncing the word "Mesopotamia" was nobody's fool; the word consists of two pure dactyls.

For an example of the satisfaction the ordinary mind takes in mere metre there is nothing better than the senseless refrains of popular songs—things which make not even the pretense of containing ideas. From the "hey ding a ding" of Shakespeare and the "luddy, fuddy," etc., of Mr. Lester Wallack's famous thieves' song in "Rosedale," to the "whack fol-de-rol" of inferior and less original composers, they are all alike in appealing to nothing in the world but the sense of time. And in this they differ in no essential particular from the verses in the newspapers; for such ideas as these contain—and God knows they are harmless—are probably never perfectly grasped by the reader, who, when he has finished his "poem," is very sure to be unable to tell you what it is all about. I have proved this by repeated experiments, and I believe I am not far wrong on the side of immoderation in saying that of every one hundred adults who can read and write with ease, there are ninety and nine to whom poetry is a sealed book—who not only do not recognize it when read, but do not understand it when pointed out. There is hardly any subject on which the ignorance of educated persons is more deep, dark, and universal. And in one sense it is hopeless. By no set instruction can a knowledge of poetry be gained. It is (to those having the capacity) a result of general refinement—the fruit of a taste and judgment that come of culture. The difficulty of imparting it is immensely enhanced by the want of a definition. If one have gift and knowledge it is easy enough to say what is poetry, but not so easy to say what poetry is.

Hunters have a saying that a deer is safe from the man that never misses. Likewise it may be said that the faultless poet gets no readers; for, as the hunter can never miss only by never firing, so the poet can avoid faults only by not writing. There is no such thing in art or letters as attainable perfection; the utmost that any man can hope to do is to make the sum and importance of his excellences so exceed the sum and importance of his faults that the general impression shall seem faultless—that the good shall divert attention from the bad in the contemplation and efface it in the recollection. In considering the character of a particular work and assigning it to its true place amongst works of similar scope and design, we must, indeed, balance merits against demerits, endeavoring in such a general way as the nature of the problem permits, to say which preponderate, and to what extent, making allowance in censure and modification in praise. But the author of the work is to be rightly judged by a different method, and he who has done great work is great, despite the number and magnitude of his failures and imperfections. These may serve to point a moral or illustrate a principle by its violation, but they do not and can not dim the glory of the better performance. Is he not a strong man who can lift a thousand pounds, notwithstanding that in acquiring the ability he failed a hundred times to lift the half of it? Who was the strongest man in the world— he who once lifted the greatest weight, or he who twice lifted the second greatest? The author of "Paradise Lost" wrote afterward "Paradise Regained." He who wrote a poem called "In Memoriam" wrote a thing called "The Northern Farmer." Of what significance is that? Shall we count also a man's washing-list against him? Suppose that Byron had not written the "Hours of Idleness"—would that have enhanced the value of "Childe Harold"? Is our hoard of Shakespearean pure gold the smaller because from the mine whence it came came also some of the base metal of "Titus Andronicus"? Surely it does not matter whether the hand that at one time wrote the lines "To Helen" was at another time writing "The Bells" or whittling a pine shingle. Literature is not like a game of billiards, in which the player is rated according to his average. In estimating the relative altitudes of mountain peaks we look no lower than their summits.

In judging men by this broader method than that which we apply to their work we do but practice that method whereby posterity arrives at judgments so just and true that in their prediction consists the whole science of criticism. To anticipate the verdict of posterity—that is all the most daring critic aspires to do, and to do that he should strive to exclude the evidence that posterity will not hear. Posterity is a tribunal in which there will be no testimony for the prosecution except what is inseparable from the strongest testimony for the defence. It will consider no man's bad work, for none will be extant. Nay, it will not even attend to the palliating or aggravating circumstances of his life and surroundings, for these too will have been forgotten; if not lost from the records they will be whelmed under mountains of similar or more important matter—Pelion upon Ossa of accumulated "literary materials."

These are points to which the critics do not sufficiently attend—do not, indeed, attend at all. They endeavor to anticipate the judgment of posterity by a method as unlike posterity's as their judgment and ingenuity can make it. They attentively study their poet's private life and his relation to the time and its events in which he lived. They go to his work for the key to his character, and return to his character for the key to his work, then ransack his correspondence for sidelights on both. They paw dusty records and forgotten archives; they thumb and dog's-ear the libraries; and he who can turn up an original document or hitherto unnoted fact exults in the possession of an advantage over his fellows that will justify the publication of another volume to befog the question. Then comes posterity, calmly overlooks the entire mass of ingenious irrelevance, fixes a tranquil eye upon those lines which the poet has inscribed the highest, and determines his mental stature as simply, as surely, and with as little assistance as Daniel discerning the hand of God in the letters blazing upon the palace wall.

II

The world is nearly all discovered, mapped, and described. In the hot hearts of two continents, and the "thrilling regions of thick-ribbed ice" about the poles, uncertainty still holds sway over a lessening domain, and there Fancy waves her joyous wing unclipped by knowledge. As in the material world, so in the world of mind. The daring incursions of conjecture have been followed and discredited by the encroachments of science, whereby the limits of the unknown have been narrowed to such mean dimensions that imagination has lost her free, exultant stride, and moves with mincing step and hesitating heart.

I do not mean to say that to-day knows much more that is worth knowing than did yesterday, but that with regard to poetry's materials—the visible and audible without us, and the emotional within—we have compelled a revelation of Nature's secrets, and found them uninteresting to the last degree. To the modern "instructed understanding" she has something of the air of a detected impostor, and her worshipers have neither the sincerity that comes from faith, nor the enthusiasm that is the speech of sincerity. The ancients not only had, as Dr. Johnson said, "the first rifling of the beauties of Nature"; they had the immensely greater art advantage of ignorance of her dull, vulgar, and hideous processes, her elaborate movements tending nowhither, and the aimless monotony of her mutations. The telescope had not pursued her to the heights, nor the microscope dragged her from her ambush. The meteorologists had not analyzed her temper, nor constructed mathematical formulæ to forecast her smiles and frowns. Mr. Edison had not arrived to show that the divine gift of speech (about the only thing that distinguishes men, parrots, and magpies from the brutes) is also an attribute of metal. In the youth of the world they had, in short, none of the disillusionizing sciences with which a critical age, delving curiously about the roots of things, has sapped the substructure of religion and art alike. I do not regret the substitution of knowledge for conjecture, and doubt for faith; I only say that it has its disadvantages, and among them we reckon the decay of poesy. In an enlightened age, Macaulay says,

Men will judge and compare; but they will not create. They will talk about the old poets, and comment on them, and to a certain extent enjoy them. But they will scarcely be able to conceive the effect which poetry produced on their ruder ancestors, the agony, the ecstasy, the plenitude of belief. The Greek rhapsodists, according to Plato, could scarce recite Homer without falling into convulsions. The Mohawk hardly feels the scalping-knife while he shouts his death-song. The power which the ancient bards of Wales and Germany exercised over their auditors seems to modern readers almost miraculous. Such feelings are very rare in a civilized community, and most rare among those who participate most in its improvements. They linger among the peasantry.

While it is true in a large sense that the world's greatest poets have lived in rude ages, when their races were not long emerged from the night of barbarism—like birds the poets sing best at sunrise—it must not be supposed that similarly favorable conditions are supplied to a rude individual intelligence in an age of polish. With a barbarous age that had recently set its face to the dawn a Joaquin Miller would have been in full sympathy, and might have interpreted its spirit in songs of exceeding splendor. But the very qualities that would have made him *en rapport* with such an era make him an isolated voice in ours; while Tennyson, the man of culture, full of the disposition of his time—albeit the same is of less adequate vitality—touches with a valid hand the harp which the other beats in vain. The altar is growing cold, the temple itself becoming a ruin; the divine mandate comes with so feeble and faltering a voice that the priest has need of a trained and practiced ear to catch it and the gift of tongues to impart its meaning to a generation concerned with the unholy things whose voice is prose. As a poetical mental attitude, that of doubt is meaner than that of faith, that of speculation less commanding than that of emotion; yet the poet of to-day must assume them, and "In Memoriam" attests the wisdom of him who "stoops to conquer"— loyally accepting the hard conditions of his epoch, and bending his corrigible genius in unquestioning assent to the three thousand and thirty-nine articles of doubt.

As inspiration grows weak and acceptance disobedient, form of delivery becomes of greater moment; in so far as it can, the munificence of manner must mitigate the poverty of matter; so it occurs that the poets of later life excel their predecessors in the delicate and difficult arts and artifices of versification as much as they fall below them in imagination and power.

1878.

The Controversialist 10:256–73.

Thought and Feeling

"What is his idea?—what thought does he express?" asks—rather loftily—a distinguished critic and professor of English literature to whom I submitted a brief poem of Mr. Loveman. I had not known that Mr. Loveman (of whom, by the way, I have not heard so much as I expect to) had tried to express a thought; I had supposed that his aim was to produce an emotion, a feeling. That is all that a poet—as a poet—can do. He may be philosopher as well as poet—may have a thought, as profound a thought as you please, but if he do not express it so as to produce an emotion in an emotional mind he has not spoken as a poet speaks. It is the philosopher's trade to make us think, the poet's to make us feel. If he is so fortunate as to have his thought, well and good; he can make us feel, with it as well as without—and without it as well as with.

One would not care to give up the philosophy that underruns so much of Shakspeare's work, but how little its occasional absence affects our delight is shown by the reading of such "nonsense verses" as the song in "As You Like It," beginning:

It was a lover and his lass,
  With a hey, and a ho, and a hey nonino.

One does not need the music; the lines sing themselves, and are full of the very spirit of poetry. What the dickens they may chance to mean is quite another matter. What is poetry, anyhow, but "glorious nonsense"? But how very glorious the nonsense happens to be! What "thought" did Ariel try to express in his songs in "The Tempest"? There is hardly the tenth part of a thought in them; yet who that has a rudimentary, or even a vestigial, susceptibility to sentiment and feeling, can read them without the thrill that is stubborn to the summoning of the profoundest reflections of Hamlet in his inkiest cloak?

Poetry may be conjoined with thought. In the great poets it commonly is—that is to say, we award the palm to him who is great in more than one direction. But the poetry is a thing apart from the thought and demanding a separate consideration. The two have no more essential connection than the temple and its granite, the statue and its bronze. Is the sculptor's work less great in the clay than it becomes in the hands of the foundry man?

No one, not the greatest poet nor the dullest critic, knows what poetry is. No man, from Milton down to the acutest and most pernicious lexicographer, has been able to define its name. To catch that butterfly the critic's net is not fine enough by much. Like electricity, it is felt, not known. If it could be known, if the secret were accessible to analysis, why, one could be taught to write poetry without having been "born unto singing."

So it happens that the most penetrating criticism must leave eternally unsaid the thing that is most worth saying. We can say of a poem as of a picture, an Ionic column, or any work of art: "It is charming!" But why and how it charms— there we are dumb, its creator no less than another.

What is it in art before which all but the unconscious peasant and the impenitent critic confess the futility of speech? Why does a certain disposition of words affect us deeply when if differently arranged to mean the same thing they stir no emotion whatever? He who can answer that has surprised the secret of the Sphinx, and after him shall be no more poetry forever!

Expound who is able the charm of these lines from "Kubla Khan":

A damsel with a dulcimer
In a vision once I saw.
It was an Abyssinian maid,
And on her dulcimer she played,
Singing of Mount Abora.

There is no "thought" here—nothing but the baldest narrative in common words arranged in their natural order; but upon whose heart-strings does not that maiden play?—and who does not adore her?

Like the entire poem of which they are a part, and like the entire product of which the poem is a part, the lines are all imagination and emotion. They address, not the intellect, but the heart. Let the analyst of poetry wrestle with them if he is eager to be thrown.

1903.

The Controversialist 10:274–77.

Visions of the Night

I hold the belief that the Gift of Dreams is a valuable literary endowment—that if by some art not now understood the elusive fancies that it supplies could be caught and fixed and made to serve we should have a literature "exceeding fair." In captivity and domestication the gift could doubtless be wonderfully improved, as animals bred to service acquire new capacities and powers. By taming our dreams we shall double our working hours and our most fruitful labor will be done in sleep. Even as matters are, Dreamland is a tributary province, as witness "Kubla Khan."

What is a dream? A loose and lawless collocation of memories—a disorderly succession of matters once present in the waking consciousness. It is a resurrection of the dead, pell-mell—ancient and modern, the just and the unjust—springing from their cracked tombs, each "in his habit as he lived," pressing forward confusedly to have an audience of the Master of the Revel, and snatching one another's garments as they run. Master? No; he has abdicated his authority and they have their will of him; his own is dead and does not rise with the rest. His judgment, too, is gone, and with it the capacity to be surprised. Pained he may be and pleased, terrified and charmed, but wonder he can not feel. The monstrous, the preposterous, the unnatural—these all are simple, right, and reasonable. The ludicrous does not amuse, nor the impossible amaze. The dreamer is your only true poet; he is "of imagination all compact."

Imagination is merely memory. Try to imagine something that you have never observed, experienced, heard of, or read about. Try to conceive an animal, for example, without body, head, limbs, or tail—a house without walls or roof. But, when awake, having assistance of will and judgment, we can somewhat control and direct; we can pick and choose from memory's store, taking that which serves, excluding, though sometimes with difficulty, what is not to the purpose; asleep, our fancies "inherit us." They come so grouped, so blended and compounded the one with another, so wrought of one another's elements, that the whole seems new; but the old familiar units of conception are there, and none beside. Waking or sleeping, we get from imagination nothing new but new adjustments: "the stuff that dreams are made on" has been gathered by the physical senses and stored in memory, as squirrels hoard nuts. But one, at least, of the senses contributes nothing to the fabric of the dream: no one ever dreamed an odor. Sight, hearing, feeling, possibly taste, are all workers, making provision for our nightly entertainment; but Sleep is without a nose. It surprises that those keen observers, the ancient poets, did not so describe the drowsy god, and that their obedient servants, the ancient sculptors, did not so represent him. Perhaps these latter worthies, working for posterity, reasoned that time and mischance would inevitably revise their work in this regard, conforming it to the facts of nature.

Who can so relate a dream that it shall seem one? No poet has so light a touch. As well try to write the music of an Æolian harp. There is a familiar species of the genus Bore (*Penetrator intolerabilis*) who having read a story—perhaps by some master of style—is at the pains elaborately to expound its plot for your edification and delight; then thinks, good soul, that now you need not read it. "Under substantially similar circumstances and conditions" (as the interstate commerce law hath it) I should not be guilty of the like offence; but I purpose herein to set forth the plots of certain dreams of my own, the "circumstances and conditions" being, as I conceive, dissimilar in this, that the dreams themselves are not accessible to the reader. In endeavoring to make record of their poorer part I do not indulge the hope of a higher success. I have no salt to put upon the tail of a dream's elusive spirit.

I was walking at dusk through a great forest of unfamiliar trees. Whence and whither I did not know. I had a sense of the vast extent of the wood, a consciousness that I was the only living thing in it. I was obsessed by some awful spell in expiation of a forgotten crime committed, as I vaguely surmised, against the sunrise. Mechanically and without hope, I moved under the arms of the giant trees along a narrow trail penetrating the haunted solitudes of the forest. I came at length to a brook that flowed darkly and sluggishly across my path, and saw that it was blood. Turning to the right, I followed it up a considerable distance, and soon came to a small circular opening in the forest, filled with a dim, unreal light, by which I saw in the center of the opening a deep tank of white marble. It was filled with blood, and the stream that I had followed up was its outlet. All round the tank, between it and the enclosing forest—a space of perhaps ten feet in breadth, paved with immense slabs of marble—were dead bodies of men—a score; though I did not count them I knew that the number had some significant and portentous relation to my crime. Possibly they marked the time, in centuries, since I had committed it. I only recognized the fitness of the number, and knew it without counting. The bodies were

naked and arranged symmetrically around the central tank,
radiating from it like spokes of a wheel. The feet were out-
ward, the heads hanging over the edge of the tank. Each lay
upon its back, its throat cut, blood slowly dripping from the
wound. I looked on all this unmoved. It was a natural and
necessary result of my offence, and did not affect me; but
there was something that filled me with apprehension and
terror—a monstrous pulsation, beating with a slow, inevita-
ble recurrence. I do not know which of the senses it ad-
dressed, or if it made its way to the consciousness through
some avenue unknown to science and experience. The piti-
less regularity of this vast rhythm was maddening. I was con-
scious that it pervaded the entire forest, and was a mani-
festation of some gigantic and implacable malevolence.

Of this dream I have no further recollection. Probably,
overcome by a terror which doubtless had its origin in the
discomfort of an impeded circulation, I cried out and was
awakened by the sound of my own voice.

The dream whose skeleton I shall now present occurred
in my early youth. I could not have been more than sixteen.
I am considerably more now, yet I recall the incidents as viv-
idly as when the vision was "of an hour's age" and I lay cow-
ering beneath the bed-covering and trembling with terror
from the memory.

I was alone on a boundless level in the night—in my bad
dreams I am always alone and it is usually night. No trees
were anywhere in sight, no habitations of men, no streams
nor hills. The earth seemed to be covered with a short,
coarse vegetation that was black and stubbly, as if the plain
had been swept by fire. My way was broken here and there as
I went forward with I know not what purpose by small pools
of water occupying shallow depressions, as if the fire had

been succeeded by rain. These pools were on every side, and
kept vanishing and appearing again, as heavy dark clouds
drove athwart those parts of the sky which they reflected,
and passing on disclosed again the steely glitter of the stars,
in whose cold light the waters shone with a black luster. My
course lay toward the west, where low along the horizon
burned a crimson light beneath long strips of cloud, giving
that effect of measureless distance that I have since learned
to look for in Doré's pictures, where every touch of his hand
has laid a portent and a curse. As I moved I saw outlined
against this uncanny background a silhouette of battlements
and towers which, expanding with every mile of my journey,
grew at last to an unthinkable height and breadth, till the
building subtended a wide angle of vision, yet seemed no
nearer than before. Heartless and hopeless I struggled on
over the blasted and forbidding plain, and still the mighty
structure grew until I could no longer compass it with a look,
and its towers shut out the stars directly overhead; then I
passed in at an open portal, between columns of cyclopean
masonry whose single stones were larger than my father's
house.

Within all was vacancy; everything was coated with the
dust of desertion. A dim light—the lawless light of dreams,
sufficient unto itself—enabled me to pass from corridor to
corridor, and from room to room, every door yielding to my
hand. In the rooms it was a long walk from wall to wall; of no
corridor did I ever reach an end. My footfalls gave out that
strange, hollow sound that is never heard but in abandoned
dwellings and tenanted tombs. For hours I wandered in this
awful solitude, conscious of a seeking purpose, yet knowing
not what I sought. At last, in what I conceived to be an ex-
treme angle of the building, I entered a room of the ordi-

nary dimensions, having a single window. Through this I saw the same crimson light still lying along the horizon in the measureless reaches of the west, like a visible doom, and knew it for the lingering fire of eternity. Looking upon the red menace of its sullen and sinister glare, there came to me the dreadful truth which years later as an extravagant fancy I endeavored to express in verse:

> Man is long ages dead in every zone,
> The angels all are gone to graves unknown;
>> The devils, too, are cold enough at last,
> And God lies dead before the great white throne!

The light was powerless to dispel the obscurity of the room, and it was some time before I discovered in the farthest angle the outlines of a bed, and approached it with a prescience of ill. I felt that here somehow the bad business of my adventure was to end with some horrible climax, yet could not resist the spell that urged me to the fulfilment. Upon the bed, partly clothed, lay the dead body of a human being. It lay upon its back, the arms straight along the sides. By bending over it, which I did with loathing but no fear, I could see that it was dreadfully decomposed. The ribs protruded from the leathern flesh; through the skin of the sunken belly could be seen the protuberances of the spine. The face was black and shriveled and the lips, drawn away from the yellow teeth, cursed it with a ghastly grin. A fulness under the closed lids seemed to indicate that the eyes had survived the general wreck; and this was true, for as I bent above them they slowly opened and gazed into mine with a tranquil, steady regard. Imagine my horror how you can— no words of mine can assist the conception; the eyes were my own! That vestigial fragment of a vanished race—that unspeakable thing which neither time nor eternity had wholly effaced—that hateful and abhorrent scrap of mortality, still sentient after death of God and the angels, was I!

There are dreams that repeat themselves. Of this class is one of my own,* which seems sufficiently singular to justify its narration, though truly I fear the reader will think the realms of sleep are anything but a happy hunting-ground for my night-wandering soul. This is not true; the greater number of my incursions into dreamland, and I suppose those of most others, are attended with the happiest results. My imagination returns to the body like a bee to the hive, loaded with spoil which, reason assisting, is transmuted to honey and stored away in the cells of memory to be a joy forever. But the dream which I am about to relate has a double character; it is strangely dreadful in the experience, but the horror it inspires is so ludicrously disproportionate to the one incident producing it, that in retrospection the fantasy amuses.

I am passing through an open glade in a thinly wooded country. Through the belt of scattered trees that bound the irregular space there are glimpses of cultivated fields and the homes of strange intelligences. It must be near daybreak, for the moon, nearly at full, is low in the west, showing blood-red through the mists with which the landscape is fantastically freaked. The grass about my feet is heavy with dew, and the whole scene is that of a morning in early summer, glimmering in the unfamiliar light of a setting full moon. Near my path is a horse, visibly and audibly cropping the herbage. It lifts its head as I am about to pass, regards me

*At my suggestion the late Flora Macdonald Shearer put this drama into sonnet form in her book of poems, *The Legend of Aulus*.

motionless for a moment, then walks toward me. It is milk-white, mild of mien and amiable in look. I say to myself: "This horse is a gentle soul," and pause to caress it. It keeps its eyes fixed upon my own, approaches and speaks to me in a human voice, with human words. This does not surprise, but terrifies, and instantly I return to this our world.

The horse always speaks my own tongue, but I never know what it says. I suppose I vanish from the land of dreams before it finishes expressing what it has in mind, leaving it, no doubt, as greatly terrified by my sudden disappearance as I by its manner of accosting me. I would give value to know the purport of its communication.

Perhaps some morning I shall understand—and return no more to this our world.

The Opinionator 10:122–33.

Wit and Humor

If without the faculty of observation one could acquire a thorough knowledge of literature, the *art* of literature, one would be astonished to learn "by report divine" how few professional writers can distinguish between one kind of writing and another. The difference between description and narration, that between a thought and a feeling, between poetry and verse, and so forth—all this is commonly imperfectly understood, even by most of those who work fairly well by intuition.

The ignorance of this sort that is most general is that of the distinction between wit and humor, albeit a thousand times expounded by impartial observers having neither. Now, it will be found that, as a rule, a shoemaker knows calfskin from sole-leather and a blacksmith can tell you wherein forging a clevis differs from shoeing a horse. He will tell you that it is his business to know such things, so he knows them. Equally and manifestly it is a writer's business to know the difference between one kind of writing and another kind, but to writers generally that advantage seems to be denied: they deny it to themselves.

I was once asked by a rather famous author why we laugh at wit. I replied: "We don't—at least those of us who understand it do not." Wit may make us smile, or make us wince, but laughter—that is the cheaper price that we pay for an inferior entertainment, namely, humor. There are persons who will laugh at anything at which they think they are expected to laugh. Having been taught that anything funny is witty, these benighted persons naturally think that anything witty is funny.

Who but a clown would laugh at the maxims of Rochefoucauld, which are as witty as anything written? Take, for example, this hackneyed epigram: "There is something in the misfortunes of our friends which we find not entirely displeasing"—I translate from memory. It is an indictment of the whole human race; not altogether true and therefore not altogether dull, with just enough of audacity to startle and just enough of paradox to charm, profoundly wise, as bleak as steel—a piece of ideal wit, as admirable as a well cut grave or the headsman's precision of stroke, and about as funny.

Take Rabelais' saying that an empty stomach has no ears. How pitilessly it displays the primitive beast alurk in us all and moved to activity by our elemental disorders, such as the daily stress of hunger! Who could laugh at the horrible disclosure, yet who forbear to smile approval of the deftness with which the animal is unjungled?

In a matter of this kind it is easier to illustrate than to define. Humor (which is not inconsistent with pathos, so nearly allied are laughter and tears) is Charles Dickens; wit is Alexander Pope. Humor is Dogberry; wit is Mercutio. Humor is "Artemus Ward," "John Phoenix," "Josh Billings," "Petroleum V. Nasby," "Orpheus C. Kerr," "Bill" Nye, "Mark Twain"—their name is legion; for wit we must brave the perils of the deep: it is "made in France" and hardly bears transportation. Nearly all Americans are humorous; if any are born witty, Heaven help them to emigrate! You shall not meet an American and talk with him two minutes but he will say something humorous; in ten days he will say nothing witty; and if he did, your own, O most witty of all possible readers, would be the only ear that would give it recognition. Humor is tolerant, tender; its ridicule caresses. Wit stabs, begs pardon—and turns the weapon in the wound. Humor is a sweet wine, wit a dry; we know which is preferred by the connoisseur. They may be mixed, forming an acceptable blend. Even Dickens could on rare occasions blend them, as when he says of some solemn ass that his ears have reached a rumor.

My conviction is that while wit is a universal tongue (which few, however, can speak) humor is everywhere a *patois* not "understanded of the people" over the province border. The best part of it—its "essential spirit and uncarnate self," is indigenous, and will not flourish in a foreign soil. The humor of one race is in some degree unintelligible to another race, and even in transit between two branches of the same race loses something of its flavor. To the American mind, for example, nothing can be more dreary and dejecting than an English comic paper; yet there is no reason to doubt that *Punch* and *Judy* and the rest of them have done much to dispel the gloom of the Englishman's brumous environment and make him realize his relationship to Man.

It may be urged that the great English humorists are as much read in this country as in their own; that Dickens, for example, has long "ruled as his demesne" the country which had the unhappiness to kindle the fires of contempt in him and Rudyard Kipling; that "the excellent Mr. Twain" has a large following beyond the Atlantic. This is true enough, but I am convinced that while the American enjoys his Dickens with sincerity, the gladness of his soul is a tempered emotion compared with that which riots in the immortal part of John Bull when that singular instrument feels the touch of the same master. That a jest of Mark Twain ever got itself all inside the four corners of an English understanding is a proposition not lightly to be accepted without hearing counsel.

The Opinionator 10:98–102.

The Passing of Satire

"Young man," said the Melancholy Author, "I do not commonly permit myself to be 'interviewed'; what paper do you represent?"

The Timorous Reporter spoke the name of the great journal that was connected with him.

"I never have heard of it," said the Melancholy Author. "I trust that it is devoted to the interests of Literature."

Assurance was given that it had a Poets' Corner and that among its regular contributors it numbered both Aurora Angelina Aylmer and Plantagenet Binks, the satirist.

"Indeed," said the great man, "you surprise me! I had supposed that satire, once so large and wholesome an element in English letters, was long dead and d—— pardon me—buried. You must bear with me if I do not concede the existence of Mr. Binks. Satire cannot co-exist with so foolish sentiments as 'the brotherhood of man,' 'the trusteeship of wealth,' moral irresponsibility, tolerance, Socialism, and the rest of it. Who can 'lash the rascals naked through the world' in an age that holds crime to be a disease, and converts the prison into a sanitarium?"

The Timorous Reporter ventured to ask if he considered crime a symptom of mental health. By way of fortifying himself for a reply, the melancholy one visited the sideboard and toped a merciless quantity of something imperfectly known to his visitor from the arid South.

"Crime, sir," said he, partly recovering, "is merely a high

degree of selfishness directed by a low degree of intelligence. If selfishness is a disease none of us is altogether well. We are all selfish, or we should not be living, but most of us have the discernment to see that our permanent advantage does not lie in gratification of our malevolence by murder, nor in augmenting our possessions by theft. Those of us who think otherwise should be assisted to a saner view by punishment. It is sad, so sad, to reflect that many of us escape it."

"But it is agreed," said the journalist, "by all our illustrious sociologists—Brand Whitlock, Clarence Darrow, Eugene Debs, and Emma Goldman—that punishment is useless, that it does not deter; and they prove it by the number of convictions recorded against individual criminals. Will you kindly say if they are right?"

"They know that punishment deters—not perfectly, for nothing is perfect, but it deters. If every human institution that lamentably fails to accomplish its full purpose is to be abolished none will remain."

The Timorous Reporter begged to be considered worthy to know what, apart from its great wisdom and interest, all this had to do with satire.

"Satire," said the Melancholy Author, "is punishment. As such it has fallen into public disfavor through disbelief in its justice and efficacy. So the rascals go unlashed. Instead of ridicule we have solemn reprobation; for wit we have 'humor'—with a slang word in the first line, two in the second, and three in the third. Why, sir, the American reading public hardly knows that there ever was a distinctive kind of writing known, technically, as satire—that it was once not only a glory to literature but, incidentally, a terror to all manner of civic and personal unworth. If we had today an Aristophanes, a Jonathan Swift, or an Alexander Pope, he would indubitably be put into a comfortable prison with all sanitary advantages, fed upon yellow-legged pullets, and ensainted by the Little Brothers of the Bad. For they would think him a thief. In the same error, the churches would pray for him and the women compete for his hand in marriage."

The thought of so great a perversion of justice overcame the creator of the vision and he sank into a chair already occupied by the cat—a contested seat.

The Timorous Reporter 10:281–84.

Preface to *Shapes of Clay*

Of the verses republished in this volume and the next, some are censorious, and in these the names of real persons are used without their consent; so it seems fit that a few words be said of the matter in sober prose. Of my motive in writing and now republishing these personal satires I do not care to make either defense or explanation, except with reference to those, who, since my first censure of them, have passed away. To one having only a reader's interest in the matter it may seem that the verses relating to those might properly have been omitted from this collection. But if these pieces, or, indeed, any considerable part of my work in literature, have the intrinsic interest, which, by this attempt to preserve some of it I have assumed, their permanent suppression is impossible; it is only a question of when and by whom they will be republished. Some one will surely search them out and put them into circulation.

I conceive it to be the right of an author to have his fugitive work in newspapers and periodicals put into a more permanent form during his lifetime if he can; and this is especially true of one whose work, necessarily engendering animosities, is peculiarly exposed to challenge as unjust. That is a charge that can best be examined before time has effaced the evidence. For the death of a man whose unworth I have affirmed, I am in no way accountable, and however sincerely I may regret his passing, I can hardly be expected to consent that it shall affect my literary fortunes. If the satirist who

does not accept the remarkable doctrine that while con-
demning a sin he should spare the sinner were bound to let
the life of his work be coterminous with that of his subject his
lot in letters were one of peculiar hardship.

Persuaded of the validity of all this, I have not hesitated to
reprint even certain "epitaphs," which, once of the living,
are now of the dead, as all the others must eventually be.
The objection inheres in all forms of applied satire—my un-
derstanding of whose laws, liberties, and limitations is at
least derived from reverent study of the masters. That in re-
spect of matters herein mentioned I have followed their
practice can be shown by abundant instance and example.

In arranging these verses for publication I have thought it
needless to classify them as "serious, " "comic," "sentimen-
tal," "satirical," and so forth. I do the reader the honor to
think that he will readily discern the character of what he is
reading, and I entertain the hope that his mood will accom-
modate itself without disappointment to that of his author.

Shapes of Clay 4:9–10.

Preface to *Black Beetles in Amber*

Most of the verses in this volume are republished from newspapers and periodicals of the Pacific Coast. Naturally, the collection includes few not relating to persons and events more or less familiar to the people of that interesting region—to whom, indeed, the volume may be considered as especially addressed, though not without a hope that its contents may be found to have a sufficient intrinsic interest to commend it to others.

In answer to the familiar criticism that the author has dealt mostly with obscure persons, "unknown to fame," he begs leave to point out that he has done what he could to lessen the force of the objection by dispelling some part of their obscurity and awarding them such fame as he was able to bestow. If the work meet with acceptance commentators will doubtless be "raised up" to give them an added distinction and make exposition of the circumstances through which they took attention, whereby the work will have a growing interest to those with the patience to wait.

Further to fortify this *apologia*, I quote from my publishers the following relevant and judicious remarks on a kind of literature that is somewhat imperfectly understood in this night of its neglect:

"In all the most famous satires in our language the victims would now be unknown were it not that they have been preserved 'in amber' by the authors. The enlightened lover of satire cares little of whom it was written, but much for what is said, and more for *how* it is said. No one but critics and commentators troubles himself as to the personality of the always obscure hero of *The Dunciad* and the nobodies distinguished by the pens of Swift, Butler, Wolcott, and the other masters of English satire; yet the work of these men is no less read than it was in their day. The same is true of Aristophanes, Horace, and the other ancient censors of men and manners."

Regarding the repeated appearance of certain offenders in the skits and drolleries of this book, I can only say that during the considerable period covered by the author's efforts to reclaim them they manifested a deplorable, and doubtless congenital, propensity to continuance in sin.

Black Beetles in Amber 5:9–10.

[On Ezra Pound]

FROM LETTER TO GEORGE STERLING:

Washington, D.C.   January 29, 1910

I'm enclosing something that will tickle you I hope—"The Ballad of the Goodly Fere." The author's father, who is something in the Mint in Philadelphia, sent me several of his son's poems that were not good; but at last came this—in manuscript, like the others. Before I could do anything with it—meanwhile wearing out the paper and the patience of my friends by reading it at them—the old man asked it back rather peremptorily. I reluctantly sent it, with a letter of high praise. The author had "placed" it in London, where it has made a heap of talk.

It has plenty of faults besides its monotonous rhyme scheme; but tell me what you think of it.

Manuscript in Berg Collection, New York Public Library; published in Bertha Clark Pope, ed., *The Letters of Ambrose Bierce* (1922; New York: Gordian Press, 1967), 158–59.

FROM LETTER TO GEORGE STERLING:

Washington, D.C.   March 7, 1910

I don't think you rightly value "The Goodly Fere." Of course no ballad written to-day can be entirely good, for it must be an imitation; it is now an unnatural form, whereas it was once a natural one. We are no longer a primitive people, and a primitive people's forms and methods are not ours. Nevertheless, this seems to me an admirable ballad, as it is given a modern to write ballads. And I think you overlook the best line: "The hounds of the crimson sky gave tongue."

The poem is complete as I sent it, and I think it stops right where and as it should—

"I ha' seen him eat o' the honey comb
Sin' they nailed him to the tree."

The current "Literary Digest" has some queer things about (and by) Pound, and "Current Literature" reprints the "Fere" with all the wrinkles ironed out of it—making a "capon priest" of it.

Manuscript in Berg Collection, New York Public Library; published in Pope, 159–60.

FROM LETTER TO SAMUEL LOVEMAN:

Washington, D.C.   March 7, 1910

These verses (which with all their faults I like) were sent to me in manuscript, but before I could do anything with them were withdrawn by the author, who had found a place for them in an English review. Since then he has published much else and made quite a little talk about himself over there and here. I think the ballad may amuse you—you need not return it.

Manuscript at University of Southern California; published in Samuel Loveman, ed., *Twenty-one Letters of Ambrose Bierce* (Cleveland: George Kirk, 1922), 17–18.

FROM LETTER TO SAMUEL LOVEMAN:

Army & Navy Club Washington, D.C.   November 27, 1910

I've not seen Ezra Pound's books, but the Goodly Fere was submitted to me in manuscript and highly commended by me. Some that were previously submitted escaped my approval by a wide margin.

Manuscript at University of Southern California; published in Loveman, 21–22.

Selected Bibliography

This bibliography contains only those entries relevant to a study of Ambrose Bierce's poetry. For more extensive bibliographies, see Grenander, *Ambrose Bierce*, 180–86; and the bibliographies in volumes 12 and 71 of the *Dictionary of Literary Biography*.

PRIMARY *(listed chronologically)*

San Francisco News Letter and California Advertiser, December 25, 1869, February 26, 1870, and March 19, 1870. These issues contain the uncollected poems "Rosalie," "To Thee, My Darling," and "Serenade."

The Dance of Death, by Ambrose Bierce and Thomas A. Harcourt, as William Herman. San Francisco: Privately printed, 1877; corrected and enlarged edition, San Francisco: Henry Keller, 1877. Satire.

Black Beetles in Amber. San Francisco: Western Authors Publishing, 1892. Revised and enlarged as volume 5 of Bierce's *Collected Works.*

Mighels, Ella Sterling. *The Story of the Files.* San Francisco: World's Fair Commission, 1893.

Stedman, Edmund Clarence, ed. *An American Anthology, 1787–1900.* Boston: Houghton Mifflin, 1900. On 443–45 are seven poems by Bierce: "The Death of Grant," "The Bride," "Another Way," "Montefiore," "Presentiment," "Creation," and "T. A. H." Although the final selection was the editor's, it was the culmination of extensive correspondence, initiated by Edwin Markham, between Stedman and Bierce.

Shapes of Clay. San Francisco: W. E. Wood, 1903. Revised and enlarged as volume 4 of Bierce's *Collected Works.*

The Cynic's Word Book. New York: Doubleday, Page, 1906; enlarged as *The Devil's Dictionary,* volume 7 of Bierce's *Collected Works.* Definitions, many with appended verses.

The Collected Works of Ambrose Bierce. 12 volumes. New York and Washington: Neale, 1909–12. In volume 1: *Ashes of the Beacon; The Land Beyond the Blow; For the Ahkoond; John Smith, Liberator; Bits of Autobiography.* 4: *Shapes of Clay, Some Antemortem Epitaphs, The Scrap Heap.* 5: *Black Beetles in Amber, The Mummery, On Stone.* 7: *The Devil's Dictionary.* 9: *Tangential Views.* 10: *The Opinionator, The Reviewer, The Controversialist, The Timorous Reporter, The March Hare.* 11: *Antepenultimata.*

San Francisco Town Talk, Sept. 10, 1910. Includes uncollected poem "My Day of Life."

Mighels, Ella Sterling, ed. *Literary California.* San Francisco: Harr Wagner, 1918.

Loveman, Samual, ed. *Twenty-one Letters of Ambrose Bierce.* Cleveland: George Kirk, 1922.

Pope, Bertha Clark, ed. *The Letters of Ambrose Bierce.* 1922; New York: Gordian Press, 1967.

Bierce, Ambrose. *An Invocation.* With a Critical Introduction by George Sterling and an Explanation by Oscar Lewis. San Francisco: Book Club of California, 1928.

Starrett, Vincent. *Ambrose Bierce: A Bibliography.* Philadelphia: Centaur Book Shop, 1929. Includes uncollected poem "How Blind Is He."

Barkin, George, ed. *The Sardonic Humor of Ambrose Bierce.* Preface by George Barkin. New York: Dover, 1963. Verse, fables, sketches, stories.

Sidney-Fryer, Donald, ed. *A Vision of Doom: Poems by Ambrose Bierce.* West Kingston, R.I.: Donald M. Grant, Publisher, 1980. Selective anthology; includes two early poems not in the *Collected Works:* "Basilica" and "A Mystery," which appeared originally in *The Californian,* Sept. 21 and Nov. 23, 1867.

SECONDARY

Aaron, Daniel. "Ambrose Bierce and the American Civil War." In *Critical Essays on Ambrose Bierce,* edited by Cathy N. Davidson. Boston: G. K. Hall, 1982, 169–81.

Aristotle. *Nichomachean Ethics.* Translated by W. D. Ross. In *The Basic Works of Aristotle,* edited by Richard McKeon. New York: Random House, 1941, 927–1112.

Brodsky, Joseph. "Poetry as a Form of Resistance to Reality." *PMLA* 107 (March 1992): 220–25.

Dickens, Charles. *The Life and Adventures of Martin Chuzzlewit,* edited by P. N. Furbank. 1843–44; Baltimore: Penguin Books, 1968.

Fatout, Paul. *Ambrose Bierce, the Devil's Lexicographer.* Norman: University of Oklahoma Press, 1951.

———. *Ambrose Bierce and the Black Hills.* Norman: University of Oklahoma Press, 1956. A detailed and authoritative account of Bierce's abortive career in mining. It involved him in protracted legal difficulties that go far to explain his numerous satires on the law, some of which are cited in this essay.

Follett, Wilson. "Ambrose Bierce: An Analysis of the Perverse Wit that Shaped His Work." *Bookman* 68 (Nov. 1928): 284–89.

———. "America's Neglected Satirist." *Dial* 65 (July 18, 1918): 49–52.

Goldstein, Jesse Sidney. "Edwin Markham, Ambrose Bierce, and 'The Man with a [*sic*] Hoe.' " *Modern Language Notes* 58 (March 1943): 165–75.

Grenander, M. E. *Ambrose Bierce.* New York: Twayne, 1971.

———. "Ambrose Bierce Describes Swinburne." *Courier* (Syracuse Univ.) 14 (Fall 1977): 22–26.

———. "Benjamin Parke Avery, California Journalist and Diplomat: Letters from Peking." *Markham Review* 2 (Sept. 1969): [4–8; unpaginated].

———. "A London Letter of Joaquin Miller to Ambrose Bierce." *Yale University Library Gazette* 46 (Oct. 1971): 109–16.

Hall, Carroll C. *Bierce and the Poe Hoax.* San Francisco: Book Club of California, 1934.

Hart, James D. *A Companion to California.* New York: Oxford University Press, 1978.

Highsmith, James Milton, "The Forms of Burlesque in *The Devil's Dictionary.*" In *Critical Essays on Ambrose Bierce,* edited by Cathy N. Davidson. Boston: G. K. Hall, 1982, 123–35.

McWilliams, Carey. Introduction to *The Devil's Dictionary,* by Ambrose Bierce. New York: Sagamore Press / American Century, 1957, v–xii.

Rather, Lois. *Bittersweet: Ambrose Bierce & Women.* Oakland: Rather Press, 1975.

Scholnick, Robert J. " 'My Humble Muse': Some New Bierce Letters." *Markham Review* 5 (Summer 1976): 71–75. Gives the background for the inclusion of Bierce's poetry in *An American Anthology,* edited by Edmund Clarence Stedman (1900).

Sheller, Harry Lynn. "The Satire of Ambrose Bierce: Its Objects, Forms, Devices, and Possible Origins." Unpublished doctoral dissertation, University of Southern California, 1945.

Sidney-Fryer, Donald. "A Visionary of Doom," Introduction to *A Vision of Doom: Poems by Ambrose Bierce.* West Kingston, R.I.: Donald M. Grant, Publisher, 1980, 9–29. Excellent study of Bierce's poetry.

Sterling, George. Introduction to *An Invocation,* by Ambrose Bierce. San Francisco: Book Club of California, 1928, ix–xvi. Discusses not only "An Invocation" but also "William F. Smith," "Another Way," "Reminded," "Presentiment," "Geotheos," "The Death of Grant," "To E. J. Salomon," "A Word to the Unwise," "The Passing Show," "T. A. H.," and "J. F. B."

Szasz, Thomas. *The Second Sin.* Garden City, N.Y.: Anchor Press / Doubleday, 1974. Szasz acknowledges his debt to Bierce as a model in the Preface, p. xv.

Title Index

Subject Index